Author is a veteran of World War II. He was appointed a sergeant by Royal Corps of Signals. He received France's highest order – Chevalier (Knight) of the Legion of Honour – by the French President during a special ceremony at Thiepval barracks in Lisburn, Co Antrim.

Neville Clifford Henshaw

FIVE UNIFORMS

AUSTIN MACAULEY PUBLISHERS™

LONDON * CAMBRIDGE * NEW YORK * SHARJAH

A CIP catalogue record for this title is available from the British Library.

ISBN 9781788486262 (Paperback)
ISBN 9781788486279 (Hardback)
ISBN 9781788486286 (E-Book)

www.austinmacauley.com

First Published (2018)
Austin Macauley Publishers Ltd.™
25 Canada Square
Canary Wharf
London
E14 5LQ

J Edgar Hoover assumes leadership of the FBI.

First photo facsimile sent, experimentally, across Atlantic by radio Mars' closest approach to Earth since 10th Century.

Failed assassination attempt on Benito Mussolini.

Malcolm Campbell sets world auto speed record at 146.16 mph.

Labour's, MacDonald government falls to Conservatives.

First, US diesel, electric locomotive enters service.

Adolf Hitler freed from jail early.

NEVILLE CLIFFORD HENSHAW BORN

Events in 1924

Baldwin government resigns.

Ramsey MacDonald forms first Labour government.

Russian city of St Petersburg renamed 'Leningrad'.

First Winter Olympic Games open in Chamonix, France.

Lenin placed in Mausoleum in Red Square.

First presidential radio address (Calvin Coolidge).

Mahatma Gandhi released from jail.

Four planes leave Seattle; on first successful round-world flight.

Test cricket debuts of Herbert Sutcliffe and Maurice Tate, v South Africa.

Ford manufactures its ten millionth, Model T, automobile.

Chapter 1

My Early Years...
How I Was a Very Rare Baby
and Met the Future King!

Any newly-born baby is, inevitably, the centre of much attention and admiration. When I came into the world, on November 9, 1924 – the fascination was greatly magnified. For I was a novelty in more than one way. I was born in Nigeria, where my parents were missionaries, and the birth of a white baby, in amongst so many black ones, was an extremely rare event. Most of the first two decades of my life were spent on Merseyside in England; but basically, I hail from Africa.

My birth place is Kwoi, a little village very close to the city of Minna, through which the main railway line travels north from Lagos. My parents – Ernest Henshaw and Georgina (nee Mortimer) – were based in Minna; both working for the Sudan Interior Mission in Nigeria. They had married in that country after relocating from Liverpool. Both had originally attended the same church in the Everton area of that city – St Benedict's; which was very much a 'young persons' church, with many opportunities to take part in various activities. In those days, with precious few alternative options, a great many young people spent a lot of time in their churches and related activities. There were no television or computer games and the likes were unimagined, and belonged very much to the future; clubs and organisations were strictly limited in number, compared with the present day.

My father was in the Boys Brigade and a member of the Church Choir. My mother was in the Girl Guides and later, after leaving school, was employed by a seamstress as a lady's dressmaker. She then began studying to become a midwife. My father left school at the age of 14 – which was nothing particularly unusual in those days – and his first employment was as an office boy with a firm of solicitors in Liverpool's Castle Street. For that, he earned the princely sum of half a crown (12½ new pence) a week. He earned promotion – and a whopping 100 per cent pay rise to five old shillings (25 pence)! However, despite these heady new salary heights, he was not happy in the work and moved to Cammell Laird Shipbuilders across the Mersey in Birkenhead. Here, he got a job in the drawing office, assisting draftsmen in drawing up plans for construction of new ships (Cammell Laird has long been one of the world's biggest names in shipbuilding and repair). His job was really only that of a general dog's body, but he still learnt a lot and enjoyed his time there.

When the First World War broke out in 1914, Dad and his two brothers – Isaac and John – went to 'join up', as most young men did. However, Dad was turned down because he was engaged in war work. Isaac was declared medically unfit, and so John was the only brother to join up. He was sent to the Royal Army Medical Corps.

The Church continued to be a big influence in Dad's life and at the end of the war, in 1918, he had the opportunity to pursue missionary work. So he eventually set off, on his own, to sail from Liverpool to Lagos on board a ship belonging to the Elder Dempster Line, another famous name in the world of shipping. In Lagos – Nigeria's principal port – there was apparently a welcoming party of native women singing and dancing. As Dad made his way down the gangway, a rather 'well-built' African lady flung her arms around him and said: (or was it 'sang'?) *ARLAFIYA*! He thought, at first, that this meant 'I love you', but he later learnt that, in the Hausa language, it just meant 'Welcome to Lagos'.

My father was then met by a young black boy who had orders to receive him and transport him in an open boat up the Niger River to Minna, where the Mission House was located. It must have been quite an adventure for my father. Until then, he had hardly ever been out of Liverpool, let alone the country – and now, here he was, aged no more than 21, suddenly on a new continent and embarking on a totally new way of life.

On arrival in Minna, there was no accommodation ready for him apart from a small African hut, with which, by all accounts, he was quite happy. He was anxious to start the work he had set out to do. He and two missionary friends began conducting their church services in – yes, an African hut, albeit a rather larger one than Dad's accommodation.

He settled down well in his new role and duly made many new friends and acquaintances. One day, one of them gave him the news that there were three young ladies who had just arrived from England – also embarking on new lives as missionaries – and that one of them had been attending the same church back in Liverpool as my father had done. They were now at a mission house some hundred miles away, but my father pricked his ears up at this and was sufficiently interested to make the long journey and meet this lady. He borrowed a rather clapped-out old motor bike for the trip – never having ridden one in his life before! He met all three of the new arrivals, but it turned out that Georgina Mortimer, my future mother, was in fact very keen to meet him because she had been told she would indeed, probably, know one of the missionaries already there.

They did know each other – at a distance – but had never been proper friends at the church back in Liverpool. Now, however, it was an altogether different matter. They got to know each other well and a full-blown relationship developed. As luck would have it, it was arranged for my mother to go and work in the same area as my father.

Once this came about, the romance simply blossomed further. My father proposed to her and she accepted. The ceremony was nothing like you might have expected back home, in England. For one thing, there were no wedding cars with white ribbons – they had to walk a couple of miles to a neighbouring village, where an ordained missionary friend was able to pronounce them man and wife. My mother also had to borrow a suitable dress to wear for the ceremony. They continued to work together – my mother was a midwife, bringing lots of black babies into the world, as well as her main missionary work – and I came onto the scene in Kwoi because my parents were working there at the time. I was later christened Neville Clifford –after my grandmother, whose maiden name was Anne Neville, and Clifford after the Governor of Nigeria, Sir Hugh Clifford.

I can't provide a detailed description of my first home – in Kwoi – but I do know that it was very primitive. It was probably little more than a glorified hut. We weren't there long, but l have been reliably informed that I caused immense interest among the locals, being the only white baby born in a land where all the rest of the new arrivals were black. Much fuss was apparently made of me!

One person who evidently was not especially interested in me, though, was none other than His Royal Highness the Prince of Wales, who, as King Edward VIII, later caused a constitutional crisis by proposing marriage to divorcee Wallis Simpson and consequently abdicating. He 'met' me on Minna Station, when he was on a royal tour of British possessions in Africa and Sir Hugh, the Governor, called my mother over, with me in her arms as a three-month-old baby, for the introduction to His Royal Highness of 'the only white baby to be born in the area'.

The story goes, however, that he wasn't at all interested in me and made it very clear that all he was concerned with was getting his hands on an ice-cold beer! Ah well, you can't win 'em all!

It's hard to realise now that I spent almost five years in Nigeria, during which time I spoke Hausa – one of Africa's largest spoken languages – fluently and English badly! That's why the friends I played with were all black children. Strange, now, to have forgotten most of my Hausa. I do remember one day asking my mother where Dad was and being told: "Oh, he's at the *By An Giddah*." In Hausa, this apparently meant he had gone to the loo! Precisely interpreted, this was 'back of the house'.

Mother, of course, was fully engaged at this time in bringing black babies into the world – although unfortunately, not for long. She suddenly became very ill with a virulent form of malaria, which was, and I believe still is, very common in that part of Africa. There are various forms of malaria – some worse than others – and some can be fatal. Another friend of my father's – a fellow missionary and a qualified doctor – advised that she needed to be taken back to Liverpool for the kind of treatment she so badly needed but which she would never find here.

So the three of us – my parents and I – returned to Merseyside, again, on an Elder Dempster vessel. My mother went into the Liverpool School of Tropical Medicine, a research and teaching institution, which had a great reputation for dealing with tropical diseases. Her treatment was indeed first class and she quickly recovered. My parents' thoughts turned to a return to Nigeria to resume their missionary work, but another friend succeeded in persuading my father otherwise, as there was a strong possibility that this form of malaria could strike my mother again if she went back.

It strikes me now that seeing Liverpool for the first time, albeit from the decks of that Elder Dempster ship, must have been quite an experience for me as a five-year-old boy. I must surely have been filled with wonderment and surprise at the sight of this thriving waterway – the River Mersey, grandly overlooked by those three imposing buildings: the Liver Buildings, surmounted by the 'Liver birds', and the two others.

Alas, and much to my regret, I have absolutely no memories of this event. Some memories become firmly printed in your mind like photographs in an album – others disappear in the mists of time.

With the help of good friends, we eventually secured a small house in Norris Green and I was duly installed in a local council school. The only thing I remember about this school is commemorating Empire Day by marching around the school yard in fancy dress (I think I wore a crown), waving Union Jacks and eventually singing *God Save the King*.

After only a short period in Norris Green, Dad was given the opportunity to move to a council house on Feltwell Road, Anfield. This was because he had recently been offered 'layman' jobs in some of the local churches. A good friend was in the process of entering the ministry of the Church of England – and he decided to follow suit. Initially, he was not too keen on the idea, feeling that he was not 'educated' enough for such a role, but it was nonetheless arranged for him to meet the Bishop of Liverpool. Bishop Martin expressed great interest in my father's work as a missionary in Nigeria.

He asked: "Have you thought of the possibility of training for the ministry?"

My father replied: "I don't think I'm up to it; I haven't got the credentials." Apparently, the Bishop dismissed this pessimism with one-word – 'nonsense'!

He added: "I have very educated men in the ministry but very few of them have the experience that you've gained in the work you've been doing."

The upshot was that my father was persuaded to enrol at St Aidan's Theological College in Birkenhead. That was quite a commitment, in more ways than one. It meant that the travelling, to and from the college each day, was quite a big undertaking. In the mornings, he would take the tram down to the Mersey. Then he would catch the ferry across the river, and I'm guessing that he would have walked the final leg to the college. Then the whole sequence would be repeated in reverse at the end of each day.

The work itself – the studying – was intense and very demanding. I know that there were occasions when he would be swotting into the early hours of the morning. It was all very worthwhile. He completed the course successfully, although it did not come easy to him, and was ordained in Liverpool Cathedral. Construction of this amazing building, which famously took many years to complete, was still under way at that time and, aged around seven, I joined my mother in a temporary structure – a bit like a football stand in appearance – erected beneath the unfinished tower. From here, we could look down on the ceremony, and I couldn't help noticing that at one stage, my father had to lie prostrate, flat on his tummy. I asked my mother, probably in a voice that was too loud for the occasion, 'why this was so'. I was absolutely fascinated by it all, but her only response was, "Ssshhhh! don't talk – be quiet!"

I remember Dad telling me afterwards that the organist was 'Goss Custard'; what a strange name for an organist, or anyone for that matter!

With my father duly ordained, he was then waiting, as they say, to be called. This wasn't long in coming – with his appointment to the curacy of the Holy Trinity Church, an old church in Liverpool city centre and now no more. Then he really 'arrived' when he became Vicar of St Polycarp's Church in the Everton area of the city. This was a very poor area at that time, but my father knew and understood it well, having been born there. Most of its residents who were employed were Dockers – and he spoke their language. He got on very well with the local people and greatly enjoyed his time there. He had never forgotten his roots there and the many friends he had made and kept in touch with.

This new beginning for Dad meant moving from Feltwell Road to St Domingo Grove in Everton and to St Polycarp's Vicarage. This was a large, four-storeyed house. To us boys, it was an exciting move. We had never lived in a house this big before.

The top floor was not used, except for storage purposes (even though there were three rooms on this level). Then there was the bedroom floor, the ground floor and lastly, 'the basement'.

It was an amazing property and one which brings back many memories. We boys used to play a lot in the basement. This consisted of a large kitchen with a 'Beeston Boiler' (it wasn't actually used as a kitchen). Above the boiler was a row of bells operated by wires, and above each bell was a number indicating from which room a bell had been rung. In the rooms, there was a handle, usually on the wall by the fireplace, which, when pulled, would sound the appropriate bell in the kitchen. Naturally, this was a source of great fascination to us and it wasn't long before my mother had to lay down the law about the ringing of those bells.

Also in the basement, there was a 'scullery' at the front of the house. This room was half under the level of the front garden (The house was built on a slope. At the back, the basement was at the ground level). In the scullery, my mother did the washing with the aid of a dolly tub and a mangle. I was usually given the job of turning the handle.

The other rooms were a toilet, wine cellar (devoid of wine), pantry and larder. This last room was later converted into an air-raid shelter. Upstairs, in the rather 'grand' hallway, we had a winding stairway leading up to the bedroom floor. The banister rail was great fun for sliding down. This was made of shiny mahogany and was frequently polished by my mother. Meanwhile, in the world of education, I was moving on …

Chapter 2

Happy Days at School...
My Uniform Number One...
The Second World War

Anfield Road Primary School was just at the end of our road. It was a steep road, as I recall, and I particularly remember 'free-wheeling' at great speed on a bicycle (not mine, actually) and suddenly jamming on the brakes at the bottom of the road. My brother, Gordon, was born there and I frequently had the unenviable job of taking him for a walk in his pram. In fact, I used to sneak into the next road, park the pram and then play football with my friends!

We were lucky to have such a good school at the end of the road. I say 'good', but it really was the most amazing school. I think it was built around the beginning of the First World War. It had three departments – the infant school (under Headmistress Mrs Marsh), the junior school, which I began to attend, and the senior school.

I started, I believe, in 1932 and I have to say, I thoroughly enjoyed school life – there was always something 'new' to be engaged in. For one thing, we had our own swimming baths, which was quite a luxury in those days. Once a week, we enjoyed a session there, with our teacher endeavouring to teach some of us actually to swim. To be honest, it was not always an enjoyable experience for me. One day, a brute of a boy decided it would be hilarious to push me in at the deep end. I couldn't swim and the teacher had no option but to jump in and rescue me! For me, all desire to learn to swim ended at that point.

The baths had a false floor that was put in place at winter time for conversion into a kind of lecture hall. We even had cinematograph shows there, usually at the end of the school year. These included such old favourites as the *Keystone Cops* and *Harold Lloyd* etc. In summertime, outdoor visits were organised. I remember going to Hooton Aerodrome in the Wirral. Two of the senior boys were given a flight in a Gloster Gladiator – lucky devils!

The time came – in the early 1930s – for me to take what was known as the Junior City Scholarship exam (the 11-Plus was still a long way off, not being created until 1944 with the Butler Education Act). This was a necessary hurdle if you wanted to move on into a grammar school. I passed, although only just, and moved to the Liverpool Institute High School for Boys in Mount Street, near the city centre, starting in the Second Form. The school was situated, in fact, right opposite the Cathedral.

(The percentage of boys transferring to grammar school at that time was not high. Most moved up into the senior school and actually received a more useful education in terms of preparing them for later life, including: joinery, plumbing and minor forms of engineering. I sometimes think I might have been better off if I had been taught joinery and carpentry instead of French and German!)

Liverpool Institute, my new school, made a big impression on me in many ways. It was a typical old-fashioned English grammar school. The main building was large and very old. It had a very big assembly hall, an equally large gallery and a huge stage. At one end of the stage was a very big, cathedral-type organ, which, I have been told, was the envy of most churches and halls in Liverpool. There was a grand piano at the other end.

Each school day began with a hymn and prayers. The headmaster, Mr J. R. Edwards, was chiefly known as 'the beak', although the older boys would also call him 'Greasy Ted'. He would sweep onto the stage for morning assembly, clad in his gown and mortar board. He would take up his position by the lectern, in the centre of the stage, and before conducting the short service, he would deftly flick his mortar board so that it would land gracefully on the piano. Accompanying on the organ was Bill Baxter, who was our Maths teacher.

I remember Mr Edwards, during one of his notices one morning, issuing the stern warning: "Boys must not frequent the fish and chipped-potato shop at the corner of the street!"

There are, of course, a great many contrasts to be drawn between the schools of my childhood and those of today, in terms of both facilities and attitudes. One such contrast that readily comes to mind concerns the seemingly ever-present debate these days over religious divisions in our schools. This simply was not an issue in my time. We didn't have any such problem. We were all catered for, very adequately and sympathetically. There were a lot of Jewish boys at my High School, but they had their own teacher and assembled in their own room for prayers and so on. It was a similar case with the Muslims.

The Liverpool Institute, on reflection, was a great school. Although I didn't realise it at the time, its traditions and strict discipline were crucial in our education and upbringing. I often wonder why I still remember most of the masters – if only by their nicknames! There was 'Biff' Bowen, for instance, who taught Maths and had a private addiction with the football pools, which he frequently mentioned.

Then there was 'Prolly' Peters, who taught History. His nickname, I think, derived from his frequent use of the word 'probably'. 'Piggy' Elliot took Geography and was such a character. He had a habit of deducting marks from your test results if you were caught chattering in class. "Boy! take two off," he would shout. Our gym master was Bertie Stell whom some of the boys, rather unkindly, renamed 'Bert the Smell'! Dan Willot taught German and his method was to speak only in that language. "Was *ist* das?" he would ask, and you had to reply in German (Fortunately, I was quite good at this subject).

Latin was another subject that was obligatory (To this day, I still wonder why). The only Latin phrase that still sticks in my mind is *'mi fili dux belli'*, which apparently means 'my son is the leader of the war'. Of course, I will never forget the school motto embroidered on our blazers: *'Non nobis solum sed toti mundo nati'* – 'we are born, not for ourselves alone, but for the whole world'. I must say that these words have grown more prophetic as I have grown older.

I used to go to school on a bicycle, which had originally been my father's. I became pals with a boy called Raymond Mellor, who lived in a house backing on to Stanley Park; we used to come home together. I was always a little envious of him because he seemed to have more stamina than I did. Our way home from the Institute took us up a very steep hill, and he would forever challenge me to ride up to the top without once getting off my bike. I would get almost to the top, only to give up because I had had enough. Of course, Ray was always able to do it, much to his smug satisfaction. I once grumbled about how tired I was, only for him to reply: "Faint heart never won fair lady!"

I didn't exactly cover myself with academic glory, but one thing I was good at was Art (as opposed to the likes of Maths – Algebra and Geometry – at which I was terrible). Art really interested me. At a Parents' Day, my mother asked Bronco Hart, my then form master, what progress I was making. He replied: "There's nothing in him." I just hope that, over the years, I have managed, in a small way, to achieve something 'in me', if only the ability to make home-made wine and grow roses!

I always associate family holidays with our stay in St Domingo Grove. At first, we used to go to Hoylake and later to West Kirby. Coincidentally, some of our neighbours used to go to Hoylake at the same time, and consequently, I would meet up with some of my pals and enjoy games on the sands. However, West Kirby was the place I liked most. We would stay in one of two 'clergy' houses – Heather Brow or Gorsebank – set in their own grounds, with swings and see-saw at the back. Ours was Heather Brow, and the two properties were entirely separate houses with a large circular lawn in front (on which we were forbidden to play!).

At the side of the front gate, there was what I can only describe as a 'castle turret' of battlements, where many games were played. First, we had to use a password, which was 'Moarty'. Nearby Caldy Hill was our favourite playing area. We also enjoyed visits to the marine lake, where we fished for crabs. These were indeed very happy days and we young ones, I suspect, were not the slightest bit concerned about the future. Alas! The future held a very dark promise. Little did we realise that in a couple of years' time, our country would be at war and that most of us would be involved in it, with some never to return.

The Liverpool Institute had an Army cadet force, as did many of the grammar schools and colleges. This aspect had taken on greater significance with the onset of the First World War (1914–18). The top public schools like Eton and Harrow had quite a reputation for their officer training corps (OTCs), with the aim of supplying commissioned officers to the Army.

We had our own OTC in our school. We were issued with a smart uniform – almost certainly a relic of the 1914–18 war and the Uniform Number One in my life – complete with peaked caps, which we nicknamed 'cheesecutters', and short jackets emblazoned with brass buttons. We called these jackets 'bum freezers'. Our legs were wound with 'puttees' (strips of khaki cloth), and our trousers, down to our ankles, were known as 'jompers'. I would have been 15 or 16 when I joined and became part of all this. We used to take part in parades, in the school grounds, about once a month. We would be dressed in our full regalia and be accompanied by our band comprising bugles and a base drum.

Once a year, we would go away on a 'field day'. This would be a whole day out, and obviously devoid of all normal school lessons. For this, we would take the Mersey railway to West Kirkby, a town on the north-west corner of the Wirral peninsula, and then march a few miles on to the village of Thurstaston. Here we would practice military manoeuvres, for want of a better term. All the way up the hill into Thurstaston, the band would be blaring away with the only tune they could play – 'All for a Shilling a Day'. We would be back in Liverpool by around 6:30 pm.

Our commanding officer was Jimmy Ledger, who taught English, and the second-in-command was 'Bronco' Hart. Jimmy was a reservist – and when the Second World War (1939–45) broke out, he was away! My own claim to any sort of honour was to pass the War Certificate

'A' Exam, which entitled me to wear a red star on my sleeve. Apparently, during the First World War, the award of this star granted the recipient a commission in the Army.

The Second World War had come ever closer, as I neared the end of my school days. Events in Europe were unfolding in unmistakably ominous fashion – leading to what would be the biggest and deadliest war in history, with over 100 million people serving in military units and resulting in up to 80 million fatalities. Soon after Britain declared war on Germany in September 1939, a major evacuation programme got under way, with children being moved out of cities and into rural areas deemed less vulnerable to attack by the German bombers.

In our family, this meant a parting of the ways from my parents for myself and my brothers – Gordon, who was seven years younger than me, and Stephen, who was five years younger than me. My youngest brother, David, who now lives in the United States, was just a baby at the time and remained at home (Stephen later died from a tumour on his parathyroid gland). Initially, we three evacuees were bound for separate locations, but we ended up all going to Southport. The Liverpool Institute was to be evacuated to Bangor, whilst the school attended by my brothers, Anfield Road, was due to go to Borth, but we never went. My mother was not happy about the splitting up and she got to know a widow in Southport, a Mrs Robb, who had already been approached to take in evacuees. So we went to live with Mrs Robb. She lived with a companion, Mrs Haslam, and employed a housekeeper called Lilly, who looked after us.

While at Southport, I attended that town's King George V Grammar School – and hated it. On the day war was declared, we boys were having our usual Sunday dinner with Lily, when we were joined by Mrs Robb and Mrs Haslam, wearing sombre expressions. Mrs Robb informed us that Mr Chamberlain, the Prime Minister, was to make an important broadcast on the wireless at midday. This information, I'm ashamed to say, made no real impact on us boys. Of much greater importance, and anticipation, at that moment was the syrup pudding we were about to consume!

I think I was, nonetheless, old enough, at 15, to appreciate the seriousness of the situation and I duly listened to Chamberlain in respectful silence: "This morning, the German ambassador was informed that unless German troops, which had invaded the territory of Poland, were removed by 11 am, a state of war would exist between Germany and the United Kingdom. I have to inform you that no such reply has been received and that consequently we are now at war with Germany."

How did this announcement affect me? Well, it certainly didn't spoil my dinner! I suppose it was a mixture of interest, fascination and even excitement. It never occurred to me then that I would be 'part of it' before very long.

Although Southport was a suburban town, appropriate preparations for its defence against air attack began to be seen in the streets, with sandbags hastily placed outside many public buildings. Men and women carrying gas masks, and some with steel helmets, were seen scurrying purposefully about town and – strangest of all – soldiers were seen dressed in a new kind of uniform and 'side caps'. Later on, I was to discover that the uniform was 'battle dress' and the hats were 'forage hats'. For some reason, this uniform was completely different from the one I had worn in the OTC.

I recall that Southport was rather a 'reserved' sort of place – a bit aristocratic, much favoured by well-heeled Liverpudlians who had chosen to retire there. Lord Street was full of small coffee shops where elderly matrons would gather on an afternoon and consume Chelsea buns and meringues whilst exchanging the latest gossip.

I wasn't there for very long. My stay was brought to an abrupt end when, after a disturbed night, I announced one morning that I didn't feel well, complaining of a sore stomach. Lily was very sceptical, but she reported the matter to Mrs Robb, who decided that I would have to be taken back home for my parents to deal with the problem. As Southport is only around 20 miles from Liverpool, this involved just a short train journey.

At first, my father suspected that I might have been trying it on, simply to get back home, and he warned me that I would be in very serious trouble if this turned out to be the case. He took me to Dr Jones, who had no hesitation in diagnosing appendicitis. I would have to go into hospital straightaway, he declared, and my father had to shut up after that. A taxi was called for and I was unceremoniously bundled into it. On arrival back home, I was confronted by my mother, carrying a bag and sporting a big smile. She reassured me that there was 'nothing to worry about'. I had expected her to be in tears, distraught. I took my essentials – pyjamas, toothbrush and so on – and was transported away in the taxi to Liverpool's Royal Infirmary. I remember being put into a large ward – and quickly concluding that I was the youngest patient there. Accordingly, I was made a fuss of by the nurses, who could only have been two or three years older than myself.

The next morning, I had the operation to remove my appendix. I was given ether gas, whilst being chatted to by a gorgeous Red Cross nurse. The operation was successful and I think I was in hospital for about ten days (How times change – now, by comparison, I would have been in and out in double quick time, just as if I were having nothing more than a tooth out). I was fortunate in that Dad, being a parson, was able to visit me frequently.

One thing I particularly remember from this experience had nothing to do with my own plight; rather, it was the sight of barrage balloons being raised all over the city, as part of the war effort, with their cables aiming to halt the German bombers (and then seeing the balloons lowered again at night). I never returned to Southport – and my two brothers also returned home by Christmas. We were not alone in doing this. A great many children were doing the same because this was the period of the 'phoney war'. Nothing was happening; the perceived threat was reduced.

Liverpool was suffering no air raids, and so, for me and my brothers at least, normal education was resumed. I returned to the Institute until I was 17, when I left school for good.

Chapter 3

**The Harsh Realities of War...
But Exciting Times for Boys**

To recall memories of the Second World War – and to make sense of it – one really has to begin with the years leading up to it. Historians, politicians and people older than I am would almost certainly say the conflict began with the Treaty of Versailles.

However, I was only a teenager, 15 years old, when war broke out, and the furthest I can go back is to events in 1938, when the seemingly distant possibility of an oncoming war was becoming increasingly evident and much talked about.

I don't remember European affairs being discussed much at the Liverpool Institute, where I was settled at this time, but certainly Herr Hitler, as he was referred to, was a sort of 'monster' in people's thoughts and minds. Like most boys, I was an avid 'doodler' and was always sketching in my books. A lot of these were of Hitler, as his distinctive appearance made him very easy to draw.

The events that stuck in my mind as a boy were the occupation of Austria and the Sudetenland and the never-to-be-forgotten announcement that Germany had no more territorial claims to make in Europe – this in the face of his famous words to the German people: *"Heute Deutchland, morgen die ganze Welt"* – Today Germany, tomorrow the whole world!

The issue that eventually brought Britain into conflict with Germany was Poland. I know that at the time there was a treaty with Poland which committed us to going to that country's aid if it was attacked, by either Russia or Germany, but I can't say I understood the treaty or why we had one. What everyone remembers from that time is Neville Chamberlain's efforts to avert war and his famous mission to meet Adolf Hitler at his mountain lair in Berchtesgaden and get him to sign a non-aggression pact.

As everyone knows, Chamberlain came back waving a piece of paper. "Peace for our time," he told the crowds at Hendon! This event, in August 1938, was almost a year before war was declared in September 1939. The mood of the country at the start of that year seemed to change dramatically. Until then, people who had shrugged off the threat of war, and who had called Winston Churchill a warmonger, suddenly had little to say. There was a general air of foreboding, and preparations and plans for war began in earnest. All sorts of instruction leaflets began to arrive in the post – how best to protect your home from bomb blasts … how to protect the windows from splintering … but the biggest paranoia was the almost inevitable acceptance that gas would be used as a weapon, and how to protect your family from such an attack.

My mother carefully read all these instructions and consequently became a mine of information. It was to serve her in good stead, because I am convinced her knowledge saved our lives, as I will recount later. In the meantime, I have no strong recollection of those spring and summer months in 1939, other than the general gloom of impending war which older people seemed to have, along with the preoccupation with events in Europe and also, to a large extent, what the politicians thought of it all.

The summer, I know, was a particularly good one. People still flocked to the beaches on the south coast in their usual numbers, despite the many preparations being made to build pill boxes and other fortifications. Barbed wire, too, was starting to appear in many places.

We, as a family, were staying at a cottage owned by a friend of Dad's. This was in North Wales, not far from Mold. There was an incident one morning, at breakfast time, when a light, single-engine RAF aircraft came flying over. Dad was watching its progress with interest when suddenly he turned to us and said: "It's coming down."

We all dashed out and saw it crash on a hedge in the field opposite. Dad and some other locals were the first on the scene. There were two men in the aircraft – a young pilot who was clearly still under instruction, and who was 'out cold', and an older man who must have been the instructor. His head was badly gashed, but he was still fully conscious and in control. I have often thought about that incident and wondered if that young pilot ended up in a Spitfire... and whether he survived.

One firm impression I have retained from the war period is that the evacuation of Liverpool was essentially a failure. I don't recall much air-raid activity affecting the city early on. The really heavy raids began at the end of 1940 and in 1941 – after most of the schoolchildren had returned! No wonder it had been referred to by some as 'the phoney war'.

The British Expeditionary Force (BEF) at this time were firmly entrenched in France, maintaining a 'line' but not in contact with the enemy. The RAF were undertaking fairly routine missions and were occasionally encountering German planes. Most of the warlike action was happening at sea, with the biggest threat coming from the German U-boats. In October, 1939, one of our largest battleships, HMS Royal Oak, was sunk by a U-boat while at anchor in Scapa Flow. The U-boat had managed to breech the defences and creep in undetected to strike the mortal blow. Nearly 800 officers and crew were lost, including a Rear Admiral. I think this action brought home to the people, at large, the fact that the war was not at all 'phoney' but deadly earnest.

My own recollections from this period – from the start of the war to leaving school at the end of 1941 – are mainly confined to the air raids on Liverpool. Nineteen-forty was chiefly memorable for the tragic retreat from Dunkirk. On the one hand, the Royal Navy, massively aided by the fleet of little boats, were eventually successful in rescuing the greater part of the BEF so that they could 'fight another day'. On the other hand, Churchill brought us down to earth by insisting that the retreat from Dunkirk was a defeat, not a victory.

From here on, there was much despondency among the British people as they came to realise the near-inevitability of Hitler and his army being free to invade our country and 'finish off the British'. The big response came in the form of the Battle of Britain, one of the greatest battles in the history of conflict. With Hitler, Goering and his lot believing we were now at our 'lowest ebb', plans for the feared invasion were undoubtedly being made by Germany. Little did they realise, however, that within the RAF, there was a new spirit prevailing. 'Stuffy' Dowding and 'Bomber' Harris had other ideas.

Squadrons of fighter aircraft, mainly comprising Spitfires and Hurricanes, took to the air to engage with the German fighters. I recall that hearing the news on the radio was a bit like listening to the cricket scores – with details every day of enemy aircraft being shot down, alongside the relatively small numbers of our own aircraft being destroyed. After a visit to a fighter station, Churchill famously remarked: "Never before in the field of human conflict, has so much been owed, by so many, to so few." These young fighter pilots were to go down in history as 'the few'.

Eventually, the German fighter war ended, despite Goering's proud boasts to Hitler. The bombers then took over, raiding our cities — London, Coventry, Manchester, Liverpool and Hull. The damage in all these cities was considerable but, though heavy, it was 'material'; it did not break the wills and minds of ordinary folk, who on the whole felt that 'bombing will never beat us'.

Night air raids did not start, as I recall, until the latter half of 1940. We had quite a few 'alerts' of short duration, when nothing much happened apart from the anti-aircraft guns firing and searchlights sweeping the sky. At the sound of the air raid alarm (dubbed 'Moaning Minnie' by my mother), we would all troop down to the air raid shelter. This was a bit cramped, having been converted from a larder. If it was late on, about 9 pm, my two brothers would be sent to bed. Mum had had the foresight to have a large old double bed installed in the kitchen. If the raid lasted late, I would join my brothers in that bed.

To me, these air raids were just pure excitement. I would sometimes stand with my father at the small side door at the front of the house. This was at the bottom of some steps in a sort of 'well', which, for some reason or other, we referred to as 'the airey' (The basement in this house was partly underground at the front and at ground level at the back). I saw flares in the sky that had been dropped by German planes, lighting up the whole area. When you saw these, you knew that bombs would soon follow. My father would make me return to the shelter and we would then hear the whistle of the bombs. You soon grasped that if you heard the whistle it meant the bomb was at least a quarter of a mile away. If it was closer, it was a completely different sound – as we discovered later on.

The planes flew over in waves and the guns would begin 'barking' away at them. We got quite good at detecting the engine note of Jerry planes, which seemed quite different from those of our own. Heavy AA (ACK ACK) guns were situated in most parks and open spaces, but there were also the mobile guns which sounded like excited terrier dogs. These had a great morale-boosting effect – it meant we were hitting back at the enemy. These guns would sometimes change their positions quite suddenly, to the point where it could sound as if they were right outside your front door!

There always seemed to be lulls in between the waves of attacking aircraft. Typically, my mother would then ask my dad to go upstairs to the kitchen to put the kettle on for a cup of tea, and I would sometimes go with him to help. One of the bright spots on these occasions was my mother producing, from nowhere, a tin of Jacobs' Custard Cream biscuits. I should add that these 'luxuries' were only made available during those air raids.

Despite everything, there were the odd humorous moments, too. My dad would suddenly giggle at Mum over a thought about a Mr Jones, who lived up the road, sitting crouched under his newly-acquired Morrison shelter. This type of shelter was constructed in the form of a dining table but made of iron. The idea was that the incumbent would be safe, sat under the table, if the house was bombed (Mr Jones was a rather tall, angular gentleman who, I think, worked in a bank).

Our closest shave came one night when, until then, nothing much had appeared to be happening. Accordingly, it was considered safer for my brothers and me to go into the big double bed, with my parents in the shelter. Suddenly, there was an almighty crash, with the sound of falling masonry and smashing glass. My parents dashed into the kitchen to see if we were okay. We were told to get dressed immediately and go to the shelter. We found everywhere covered in a fog of thick dust and there was a strong, acrid smell. We boys were in a bit of a daze, as we had been fast asleep. Brother Stephen managed to get both his legs stuck in one leg of his shorts, with him consequently 'hopping' to the shelter.

A bomb had landed right in between our house and the next one. It demolished the whole corner of the house next door. This left the bathroom open to the elements and its toilet bowl dangling freely – of which I still have a snapshot! It also demolished the annexe to our house. This contained a cloakroom upstairs and a WC underneath. My parents feared that the house might come tumbling down on top of us, but we were lucky. Ours was a fairly old, stone-built, four-storey structure. Had it been more like the one next door, things could have been very different.

My mother's foresight in building a 'retaining' wall of sandbags outside our shelter certainly paid off. The bomb caused a big crater, which itself threw up a lot of soil against those sandbags. The people next door were also very lucky. They were in their Anderson shelter at the bottom of their garden. To us boys – again – all this was great excitement. It was something we could boast about at school, and we scrambled around in the crater, eagerly seeking bits of bomb shrapnel. My father later reflected that the bomb had sounded like an express train emerging from a tunnel. Apparently, he had shouted at my mother: "This one's for us." He had grabbed her forcibly and pulled her onto the floor. We all survived and, what's more, we had great fun recounting the tale afterwards.

Chapter 4

Air Raids Increase...
I Leave School...
My Uniform Number Two

The air raids became much more ferocious in 1941 – which was my last year at school, with me now 16. The Luftwaffe sent larger numbers of planes, and their bombs were heavier and more damaging. Two new weapons were being used as well – the land mine and the incendiary bomb. Land mines were dropped by parachute and sometimes caught in trees and telegraph wires. They did much damage, flattening large areas. The incendiary bombs, if I recall correctly, were about 14 inches long and 2½ inches wide. They burst a few seconds after impact. If you got to them quickly enough, they could easily be doused with a shovel full of soil or sand.

In one night raid, two of these bombs landed in our back garden. A neighbour, sheltering with us at the time, went out with my father and together they were able to extinguish them in time. I had planned to use the stirrup pump and was a bit miffed at not being able to do so!

Around this time, shops, offices, schools and churches organised themselves into teams of firewatchers. This was principally to protect buildings from those incendiary bombs. In our school, boys over 16 were invited to volunteer for such duty. A fire-watching team consisted of two masters and two boys. We would be given an evening meal, prepared by the school chef, and breakfast the next morning. The boys would occupy the masters' common room and the masters, the Headmaster's private rooms.

I didn't see much action during my spells of duty, but some boys did. In the worst fire raid over Liverpool, some incendiary bombs landed on the school roof, but they were quickly kicked down on to the school yard below, where they did little damage.

I believe it was during this same night that Liverpool's large Lewis's store was tragically bombed. Fire bombs had already started a fire and firewatchers were on the roof. A large high-explosive bomb then landed, entering the lift shaft and exploding several floors below. Despite frantic rescue attempts, I believe none of those firewatchers survived.

In another incident – again, possibly the same night – bombs landed in an ammunition train in a siding at the docks. A potential disaster was averted by the courageous engine driver who, without thought for his own safety, shunted the train away from the highly populated area to one of relative safety. I don't know if he was hurt, but I believe he was honoured with the George Medal.

In the May blitz of 1941, Liverpool was bombed for eight consecutive nights. Each night, the air raid warning would sound at 6 pm and the 'all-clear' would not be heard until some 12 hours later. I can clearly remember beautiful, warm summer weather, with my mum typically pottering about in the front garden of an evening, when the alarm would go. On one such evening, she was chatting to a neighbour – a cheerful fellow who was going on night duty at Mill Road Hospital, where I think he was a porter. That was the last we saw of him. He was killed that night in the operating theatre of the hospital, which suffered a direct hit from a land mine. Apparently, the entire theatre team were killed outright, along with the patient.

As air raids became part and parcel of our daily lives, so we actually became quite blasé about them. It's amazing, really, how easily people can adapt to situations – ANY situations. In the event, I think 1941 also saw the last of the big raids. It seemed Gerry had finally realised there wasn't much future in trying to bomb the British into submission. After all, our own RAF were mounting reprisal raids on German cities with frightening effect. Some of the damage caused was far greater than that inflicted on our own cities. Dresden was a case in point, and many questions have since been raised as to whether these reprisals were justified.

I left school at Christmas, 1941, with, I'm afraid, no scholastic honours. There were quite a lot of jobs being advertised for the Civil Service, and I was fortunate enough to secure one of these. This was in the Ministry of Supply, as a temporary clerk (Grade III), and I found myself working in Liverpool's famous Liver Buildings on the waterfront. I was based in the top floor, and it was a new experience which I enjoyed immensely. The work was relatively simple. We were responsible for processing bills received from armament firms for ammunition supplied to the forces.

Working with me were quite a lot of young people around my own age, and I made many new friends.

Dinner hours were always pleasant. In bad weather, a few of us would go to a recreation room where there was a radiogram. One of our female colleagues would teach us ballroom dancing – which is where I learnt how to dance, after a fashion! When the weather was good, we would stroll down to Liverpool's Landing Stage.

The Mersey was always a hive of activity, with troopships taking on troops bound for distant shores and, frequently, convoys with their escort vessels just arriving from America.

Another favourite pastime was to go up onto the roof of the Liver Buildings, with its great view of the river and the Wirral peninsula (There was also a good view of the girls who liked to go up there to sunbathe). There was no staff canteen, so you either brought your own sandwiches or went to a restaurant. I used to go to an eating house called George Petty's. There was another, cheaper establishment run by a brother – Harry Petty's – and this was frequented mainly by office boys. My dad went there when he was a boy.

He would tell me how they sold rice pudding in a solid block. They would out a slice and put condensed milk on it, and this cost one (old) penny! George Petty's was far more sophisticated. We enjoyed a three-course dinner for 1s 6d on days when they had steak pie with 'real steak' (only given to regulars). Then the cost was 1s 11d – rather dear!

Our department, which was known as SF4K, was a bit like a transit camp. Young chaps – and a few girls – were leaving almost every week to go into the forces. There would be collections for all the departing 'conscripts', to which we all had to contribute. The money would usually be collected mid-afternoon by the department head, and the recipient was obliged to supply cakes to go with the tea break!

In early 1942, I joined the Home Guard, which had just had its name changed from the Local Defence Volunteers (LDV). My company was situated on the side of Stanley Park. On my first day, I was shown into a room with a stack of used uniforms. I was told to sort one out for myself – the Uniform Number Two in my life – my eventual choice was far too big, but I just had to 'lump it'.

I wasn't in the Home Guard for very long – only about a year – but during that time, I picked up more of the rudiments of military education. I learnt how to fire a rifle and do various mundane jobs. I also took part in a three-day exercise. For my guard duty, my sentry box was in the back garden, facing the park. We were billeted in an old mill close to Aintree Racecourse and had to sleep on the floor. I think I had to do messenger duties.

Then, once I was 18, came 'the real thing'. All too soon, the fateful day arrived when I got my official call-up, which happened to us all, provided we were healthy. I received a 'summons' to attend an Army medical examination which, I think, was held in the Central Hall in Liverpool. We were shunted around various booths with rather bored-looking doctors poking and prodding our bodies, presumably looking for some reaction. I was graded A1, along with just about everyone else, so far as I recall. This meant that I had been pronounced fit to join the forces – and to fight for King and County.

Chapter 5

Army Life Takes over...
My Uniform Number Three...
The D-Day Landings

With receipt of my call-up papers, I was to report to a general service battalion at Ben/Vick-on-Tweed, on the border with Scotland, on March 3, 1943. I duly left the Ministry of Supply with the usual presentation – a silver cigarette box – and the custom of supplying those cakes for the tea break. Finally, the day came for me to leave home, not without a certain trepidation, and leading to my Uniform Number Three, of course. Dad came with me to Lime Street Station and got me settled on a train. He said little, just patted me on the shoulder and said: "Don't forget to write to your mother." As he walked away down the platform, in his dirty old raincoat, he turned once, waved, and was gone. I was never an emotional boy, but right then, it was mighty hard to keep the tears at bay.

As the whistle blew and the train began to pull away, I was aware of a rather skinny lad entering my carriage. He looked at me and, in a strong scouse accent, asked: "Any seats there, Whack?" I indicated the window seat opposite me. We got talking and he asked where I was off to. I told him and he said that was where he was going, too! So, that journey was accompanied by plenty of chatter!

We finally arrived at Ben/Vick-on-Tweed in the early evening. We were a rather motley crew, suddenly brought together by a fearsome drill sergeant wearing a red sash and barking out unintelligible commands. We were bundled into a foul-smelling lorry and whisked off to the camp. This was actually positioned in Scotland (with Ben/Vick-on-Tweed being in England – a border town with ancient walls). On arrival, we were directed to a barrack hut and informed that this was to be our new living quarters. We had no beds. Instead, we were issued with hessian sacks and told to go to the back of the hut, where there was a pile of straw – with which we could fill our sacks. ("This is the Army, Mr Jones.")

For the next few weeks, we didn't know whether we were coming or going. We had a lot of 'square bashing' (drill on the barracks square), endured countless personal insults and learnt the innards of an SMLE (Short Magazine Lee Enfield rifle). We learnt how to throw a hand grenade (could be tricky!) and were taken into trenches, where we had to throw the grenade over the top as far as we could. A colleague only just cleared the parapet – with the grenade rolling lazily back into the trench and exploding! Luckily, the sergeant in charge spotted the danger, grabbed him and hauled him to safety. His language at that point was very colourful, with unmistakable references to the poor lad's parentage.

We were also taken to the firing range, where, I must say, I acquitted myself fairly well. At least I managed to hit the target. Towards the end of our training period, suffered the rigours of the assault course. This involved scaling a 6ft wall, scrambling down cliffs to a rocky shore below, proceeding along rocks for about 100 yards, and then climbing back up cliffs and proceeding across a field to the finish. I wasn't among the first, but nor was I the last!

An interview with a panel of red-tabbed officers determined which arm of the services we were to be sent to. For me, it was to be the Royal Corps of Signals, reporting to a Signals unit in Chester. Here I was to be trained as a teleprinter operator, or to be exact an 'operator keyboard and line' (OKLBIII). On arrival, we were surprised to discover that ATS girls were to train us in the keyboard skills – and I'm pleased to confirm that these skills were not the only ones they passed on! I never really got the hang of touch-typing, but amazingly, I passed the test and became an OKLBIIII.

I was then posted to an L of C unit (Line of Communication) at Thirsk in Yorkshire. Here I managed to click with a girl called Dorothy, who worked at a grocer's shop in the village. She would treat me to chocolate biscuits from the shop – bearing in mind that these were a great luxury in the war. Her parents were chicken farmers and she took me to meet them. I was given a tour of the farm, although this failed to impress me. I did get the chance to take Dorothy for a walk, although that, quite literally, was as far as it went. We weren't long in Thirsk, but one memory is of our sergeant major, a small Welshman, stopping directly behind me and enquiring: "Am I hurting you, ladder?"

I replied: "No, Sir."

In a strong Welsh accent, he countered: "Well, I ought to be. I'm standing on your hair. GET IT CUT."

I was promoted to Lance Corporal and detailed to take a section of men to be billeted in a disused brewery that was infested with rats. We arrived to discover no bunks, so had to sleep on the floorboards. I found five beer crates and was able to make a sort of bed out of these. What sleep we managed was shattered in the middle of the night by an unearthly scream – one of the men had been bitten on his neck by a rat! I quickly got him to the medical officer, but the main artery had not been punctured – the poor man had just suffered a scratch.

After Thirsk, I was sent to various camps across England – Huddersfield, Putney, Barnet and finally Potters Bar, where, to my disgrace, I was demoted to signalman after a humiliating incident involving the sentry box guard. One night, I was guard commander and one of the men, known to be soft in the head, was on sentry duty. The sentry box was at the entrance to the delivery yard at the rear of the shops, with one of them serving as the guard house. From the guard house itself, you could not see the sentry box.

In the early hours of the morning, the door burst open and the duty officer, in a rasping voice, asked: "Where the hell is your sentry?"

"He's in the s-sentry box," I stuttered.

"Oh no he bloody well isn't," said the officer, adding: "But his rifle is propped up on its own there. COME WITH ME."

I did as instructed and when passing the back of a shop that our unit was using as a mess room, I noticed the light was on – and there was the missing sentry, eating something.

Consequently, this idiot was up before the commanding officer on a charge and given 28 days 'CB' (confined to barracks). I was also 'up' and, to my everlasting shame, was demoted back to signalman. I'm glad to say that I did eventually get my stripe back.

At Potters Bar, I had weekend passes into London. There were a lot of forces canteens catering for troops from all over the world and a member of the forces could enjoy a very cheap outing in the Metropolis. One club we used to go to (which was free to enter and with cheap refreshments) put on a radio show every Saturday – I think it was 'Variety Band Box'. Some very big stars appeared on it, including Bing Crosby and Bob Hope. It was free to get in and refreshments were cheap. I saw both Bing and Bob in special concerts for members of the Forces – Bob Hope was particularly funny and popular.

During one London visit, I got caught up in a 'doodle bug' raid. These were bombs, radio-controlled and launched from the German coast. I was with a companion in Regents Park when this thing flew over us. We knew that when the engine cut out, it would begin its dive and that's exactly what happened; luckily, it landed some distance away – about 100 yards – with a mighty explosion.

Another time, we were in the Tower of London, being escorted by a 'Beefeater' whose impromptu commentary would have done any TV presentation proud. It was something like this: "And over there, in the middle of the courtyard is where Anne Boleyn was beheaded, and if you look upwards towards the corner of the White Tower, you will see a doodle bug heading this way and I hope you will excuse me when I request that you take cover, immediately." Cue consternation, at least among many of the foreign visitors.

The invasion of Europe, or the 'second front', as it was generally known, was about to begin and we would soon be an integral part of it. I think the first indication that something was about to happen was when we received orders to paint all vehicles with identification marks. Nobody really knew where we were going. Then, quite suddenly, we were on the move. We arrived at a camp on Salisbury Plains; from the outset, strict security was enforced. We were not allowed out of the camp and were forbidden to write letters home. Instead, we were given little buff cards which briefly explained our situation without giving away any details.

We were in that camp for about a week and then – again, very suddenly – we were on the move once more. Northerners like me had no idea where we were; we had to rely on the few southerners, who assured us that we were heading for Southampton. It seemed obvious that we were being sent to the Far East, but this was not so. We eventually arrived at Gosport, near Portsmouth, on June 1, and were billeted in an empty school (most schools in the area having been evacuated to rural villages). We were not told our eventual destination, although we had a gut feeling that the officers knew. For the next few days, we were kept occupied with route marches and PT sessions, interspersed with rifle drill.

None of us really had any idea what was going on around our own little world, still less that the D-Day landings were imminent! On June 4, we were marched to the harbour to board an LST (Landing Ship Tank). The smell of that vessel – the all-pervading stink of diesel – is still with me to this day! We were issued with waxed boxes which, we were told, contained emergency rations, along with instructions not to open them until we arrived at our destination. There was no 'comfort' on this boat – nowhere to sit. We just had to park ourselves on the deck as best we could. But then, before we had set sail, we were suddenly ordered to disembark and return to our billet. Talk about the grand old Duke of York!

Back at the school, our officer explained that bad weather had postponed our operation. Cue much muttering and grumbling, and some of the lads began singing, "Abbie, Abbie, Abbie my boy, what are we waiting for now?" The good news was that we got a good dinner that night, but with warnings to get to bed early. We had to be up at 5 am next morning. That next day, it was back to the harbour and boarding the same smelly boat. Once again, it was the waiting game –

all day, in fact – but come evening, we heard the engines starting up. At last, the LST moved slowly away from the harbour, heading towards the Isle of Wight and eventually entering the English Channel.

Darkness was descending and myriad twinkling lights could be seen on either side of us. I often reflected on the wonder that Gerry didn't mount a fierce attack on us at that point (although I believe there was a small attack by patrol boats further down the Channel). The weather was still bad and some of the lads were seasick; I didn't feel great but managed to avoid vomiting. The noise of aircraft was incessant and we could hear the sound of heavy guns from the French coast – but could see very little. The men's chattering – and the wisecracks – had stopped now.

As we got nearer, we could make out the French coast and signs of explosions. We anchored for a short while and our officer pointed out where we were to land. Our beach was codenamed 'Gold'. We lined up in a sort of queue and any remaining doubts that this was now very much the 'real thing' were shattered when a landing ship to our starboard side suffered a direct hit and began to sink. There's no denying that this scared the living daylights out of us.

Finally, we made our run up to the beach, but there was still over a foot of water when we grounded. I jumped from our LST but slipped and briefly 'went under'. So I was immediately drenched from head to toe. Someone grabbed me by the scruff of the neck and hauled me out.

A voice yelled: "Get the hell out of here, quick." Our officer had already pointed out to us a blown-up tank – one of ours – half-way up the beach. Here he suggested we take a breather. A few of us scrambled towards the remains of that tank and flopped down behind it.

Then some maniac of a sergeant screamed: "You will all be dead if you stay there; get the hell out of it."

So we started stumbling towards the sand dunes, convinced the end was just moments away. We mumbled prayers and – yes – I wondered what my mother would say. But some of us did make it, including myself, albeit being very aware that something like ten per cent of our unit were not so lucky. The lucky ones were able to take cover in a badly shelled building. Our officer decided that this was a suitable position to set up a signal station to communicate with the various headquarters in 21st Army Group.

He also told us that we were unlikely to receive any rations for a couple of days, and so we could open our 'emergency' rations, contained in a waxed box, of about 4x6 inches, held in the trouser pocket. Inside were two dried blocks – one of minced meat and the other of porridge. There were also boiled sweets, chocolates and a few cigarettes – not forgetting, placed neatly on top of these, all of three sheets of toilet paper! I will always remember two guys opening these boxes and one saying: "Three sheets of bog roll, that's not much use." and the other replying: "What are you 'binding' about? There's one for up, one for down, and the other one for polishing!" Then we had to get cracking in sending and receiving messages on our radios. Later on, we were issued with teleprinters that afforded more efficient communications.

A well-known book about D-Day was entitled *The Longest Day*, which was an apt title. It certainly was a long day. When nightfall finally arrived, we were subjected to a raid by German dive bombers – the Stukas. Luckily, they didn't get us. We were eventually on the move up Bayeux Road, but only a couple of miles further on. The forward troops of 2nd Army under Dempsey had captured Bayeux, whilst our signals unit had taken over a large field. I was a lance corporal at this time and, together with two erks, was given the job of constructing a urinal. We had to dig a hole and a bucket, with holes in the bottom, had to be pushed at an angle into the hole. Then four posts were dug in and covered with tarpaulin. I was quite proud of the result and, being in charge, was given the honour of christening it in the customary manner!

Neville lays the Wreath at the United Remembrance Day
Sunday 8th November 2009

SUPREME HEADQUARTERS
ALLIED EXPEDITIONARY FORCE

Soldiers, Sailors and Airmen of the Allied Expeditionary Force!

You are about to embark upon the Great Crusade, toward which we have striven these many months. The eyes of the world are upon you. The hopes and prayers of liberty loving people everywhere march with you. In company with our brave Allies and brothers-in-arms on other Fronts, you will bring about the destruction of the German war machine, the elimination of Nazi tyranny over the oppressed peoples of Europe, and security for ourselves in a free world.

Your task will not be an easy one. Your enemy is well trained, well equipped and battle-hardened. He will fight savagely.

But this is the year 1944 ! Much has happened since the Nazi triumphs of 1940-41. The United Nations have inflicted upon the Germans great defeats, in open battle, man to man. Our air offensive has seriously reduced their strength in the air and their capacity to wage war on the ground. Our Home Fronts have given us an overwhelming superiority in weapons and munitions of war, and placed at our disposal great reserves of trained fighting men. The tide has turned ! The free men of the world are marching together to Victory !

I have full confidence in your courage, devotion to duty and skill in battle. We will accept nothing less than full Victory !

Good Luck ! And let us all beseech the blessing of Almighty God upon this great and noble undertaking.

Dwight D Eisenhower

"Fine words – ahead of fine deeds."

This was the stirring message to the
soldiers, sailors and airmen of the Allied Expeditionary Force, on the
eve of the D-Day Landings, delivered by General Dwight D. Eisenhower,
the Force's Supreme Commander.

HRH the Prince of Wales (later known as The Duke of Windsor) at Minna Station, Central Nigeria, during his tour of British countries in Africa.

My mother, before I was born, on her arrival as a Missionary in Nigeria, circa early 1923

My mother and father's wedding at Minna, Central Nigeria, circa late 1923

My mother holding me, a few weeks old

Me with my 'girlfriend' in Minna, circa 1927

With my best pal in Minna, circa 1927.

Mother and Dad – now a Vicar in the Church of England in Liverpool –
Circa 1937.

Chapter 6

Constantly on the Move...
Some More Awful Experiences...
But All Bad Things...
Come to an End

The battle moved on, leaving us behind to become a small part of the communications network. The horrific battles of Falaise and Caen were fought against very strong German resistance; we were lucky not to be part of this, I suppose. Caen was a sea of rubble; when I had to go there with an officer to contact a signal unit. The only building still standing, it seemed, was the castle (William the Conqueror's home), following a heavy RAF raid.

We remained in the area for two months and were then moved on to Ghent in Belgium, arriving shortly after its capture by the allies. There was no shortage of affection shown towards us British soldiers by the town's female population, and a lot of the boys took full advantage! We had not been in Ghent for very long when a few of us were sent on detached duty to an RAF Air Sea Rescue unit in Ostend, and this gave me altogether more pleasant memories than those of D-Day.

We occupied a former small hotel, but before we could enter it, some Canadian engineers had to clear it for booby traps. The town had only recently been captured by the Canadian 3rd Division and apparently Gerry had left a lot of mines and booby traps all over the place. A booby trap was discovered in our building, attached to the flush chain in a toilet. I can only imagine that there was a weird sense of humour behind this. One of our chaps remarked that it would have been a great cure for constipation, but it was a good job that none of us was 'dying to go'. Whatever else may have been lost, humour lived on!

We set up an RAF signal office in Ostend and were attached to their Air Sea Rescue unit, comprising a fleet of motor torpedo boats. Their task was to rescue pilots and crew from planes that had crashed in the English Channel. Our unit was a detachment of the 17th Air Formation Signals, led by Sergeant Joe Usher. Our team consisted of four teleprinter operators, including myself, four 'linesmen' and one IM (instrument mechanic). We operators also had to operate a 40-line FF switchboard (field and fortress).

We worked a three-legged watch system. Night was always very busy on the teleprinter, strangely enough, but the switchboard got fairly quiet after midnight, and we would get our heads down alongside it. There was a night alarm in place, but it wasn't very loud. One of us complained to Sid Vining, the instrument mechanic, who said, "leave it to me." The next night, at about 3 am (I was off duty), there was an earth-shattering clanging, waking the entire house and RAF HQ on the other side of the road. Sid was overcome with hilarity – but others among us were not amused!

While in Ostend, there was a hairy incident when I had to go with the Linesmen to do a job on fallen lines. One of their men was sick and I was supposed to be off duty. The line fault was somewhere up the coast, short of Antwerp. Suddenly, there was a huge explosion and I was propelled skywards out of the Jeep, landing in a field. I was shocked but not seriously injured. I lay there, stunned, for a while and then heard English voices. It was an Army patrol, who swiftly got us – me and two others – back to a field hospital in Ostend. The Jeep had apparently driven over a 'teller mine', a German-made anti-tank mine common in the Second World War. I quickly recovered and life for me in the RAF Signal Office resumed as normal. That was the way of things – you just had to 'carry on'.

Our billet was in fact pretty comfortable. With two other chaps, Gerry West and Alf Button, I occupied a room on the top floor. We worked shifts but in between had free periods. At a dance, I and someone else got friendly with two Belgian girls. Mine was called Georgette. I dated her and took her out on a rowing boat on a park lake. She was a nervous creature and sat apart from me at the far end of the boat. She need not have worried because I had no seduction plans in mind!

We returned to Ghent, where the rest of our company was but this was short-lived as we received orders to join up with 30 Corps 2nd Army in its advance to relieve the airborne boys at Arnhem – which, as famously depicted in the film *A Bridge Too Far*, we failed to do (although to be fair I think we were let down by poor intelligence).

At this stage of the war, the Germans were fighting desperately and bravely. Of course, they were hampered by Hitler's leadership. The fighting in the Reich Wald Forest was particularly bitter and we lost some good men there. However, the German Army was finally forced to pull back over the Rhine, and for the first time we were fighting Gerry on his own territory. The Germans, from top to bottom, were beginning to realise that it was all over bar the shouting. Nonetheless, a last-ditch undercover force known as 'werewolves' began setting up all sorts of traps for the incoming British and American forces. A favourite trick was to stretch piano wire across a road. This would decapitate anyone on a motor bike, such as an Army dispatch rider. One of our own men died in this way.

Our next move was to Schloss Bruhl near Cologne on the Rhine. Bruhl was in an American sector and we were temporarily attached to an American unit. We had to man a switchboard on their behalf. We enjoyed American rations – which were considerably superior to ours. We got a lot of tinned fruit and, something completely new to us, peanut butter. I was in the advance party, and the Americans allocated to us houses previously occupied by Nazi party officials. They had evidently left in a hurry, with furniture, carpets and curtains all still in place. There were also large stocks of preserved food in the cellars, along with wine and spirits. The first night we were there, we had a ball! We all got fairly drunk on Moselle Wein. I slept it off in a big double bed, covered by a huge feather quilt. This was really living! It was my first night in a bed since I was last home on leave.

After a typically short stay in Bruhl, we were shunted off to a little German village rejoicing in the name of Wellingholzhausen, somewhere near Osnabruck. Why we were sent there, I don't know! I do remember befriending two German brothers, Jurgen and Manfried. Like many German boys then, they were keen to work for us for coffee, cigarettes and chocolate. They took my washing and then even took me to their home to meet their parents. Their father, who had been an officer in the Panzer regiment, had just been released by the British after being taken prisoner. It was a strange meeting. They were really very friendly people, with no acrimony or coolness. At that time, British soldiers were not allowed out of camp without arms. I had a rifle over my shoulder. I placed it between my knees while I accepted my hosts' acorn coffee. I left shaking hands with the boys' father, my former enemy.

Our stay in Wellingholzhausen ended abruptly. German resistance lessened and finally ended. Celebrations soon followed on VE Day (Victory in Europe). Our unit was posted to Bury in Lancashire and we took part in a victory parade through Manchester, receiving a great reception. Shortly afterwards, and again quite unexpectedly, we were given embarkation leave, being sent to the Middle East. We were soon on board a troop ship bound for Egypt.

During a very pleasant voyage, we called into Gibraltar and Malta before arriving in Port Said, anchoring outside for the best part of a day while we awaited a berth. The local 'wogs' (westernised Oriental gentlemen!) rowed out in their boats offering all sorts of leather goods for sale. This was done with a basket and a long length of rope thrown up on to the ship's deck to be secured, with the other end tied to a basket. You pointed out something you fancied, negotiated a price and threw the money down into the boat, with the goods then hauled up in the basket. And of course it was all rubbish!

A train took us to our base at Quasasin, way out in the desert. We lived under canvas, covered in mosquito nets, but were soon sent on to Maadi, just south of Cairo. It was on the fringe of the desert, but populated mainly by French and other Europeans. There were some lovely houses, gardens and a golf course, plus an Anglican church. Altogether, I was in Egypt from 1946–47. I managed to visit the Pyramids and the Sphinx, but would have made so much more of them if I had then the abiding interest in medieval history that I now have.

Other shore leave spells included a visit to Lake Timsah, an offshoot of the Suez Canal. This was a sort of mini resort, where you could swim and dive. To begin with, I could not swim. So I just hopped around in the water on one leg, making suitable movements with my arms. Then I suddenly realised my one leg wasn't touching the bottom anymore – I was swimming, after a fashion! A pal challenged me to swim out to a raft that was in 20 feet of water. I managed this, with him alongside me, and he then told me to return unaccompanied!

During our final location in Egypt, at El Ballah on the banks of the Suez Canal, I was promoted to sergeant and at the same time given the job of 'education sergeant' for the battalion. I had a small team of instructors, and a library. I gave lectures and, in the evenings, gramophone recitals of classical music. I had my own office and a motor bike! I was sent on an instructors' course to Haifa in Palestine. The officer sat next to me in the classroom was Lieutenant Lord Balneil, who was later one of Princess Margaret's consorts. He was a nice chap – and constantly looked over my shoulder to see what I had written!

Palestine was in the throes of terrorism against the British. During my stay there, there was a particularly nasty incident just south of Haifa, with two British soldiers abducted and hanged in an orchard. Another party of soldiers were swimming at a beach when they were all machine-gunned to death. One night on Mount Carmel, where our course was being held, we heard big explosions and saw three oil tankers on fire in the bay – more victims of terrorism.

Once demobilisation was under way, each of us was allotted a number indicating our position in the general demob order. Mine was 52, which meant a long wait. The day finally came and I found myself on Ismalia Station, waiting for the train to Port Said, where we were sent first to a holding station. After about three days there, a Liverpool-bound troopship came in and we were herded aboard. By now, something of a holiday atmosphere prevailed.

We arrived in the Mersey late at night, on June 7, 1947. We anchored at The Bar and I did 'picket' duty – my last military duty in the Army. The next day, we berthed at the Landing Stage and – a memory still so clear – I spotted my father waiting for me down below, among hundreds of others. He soon spotted me and shouted up: "When will you be home?" A thousand voices answered him! We boarded a train for York, where there was a demob centre and where I enjoyed one of my best-ever Army meals.

The next day we were taken to a clothes store, where we had to choose a suit, two shirts and, I think, a pair of shoes. Railway warrants were issued, plus Army 'pay' – and that was it! Thus ended four-and-a-half years' military service. I returned to Liverpool by train and was back home by tea-time. I slept badly that first night – just couldn't get used to the comfortable bed and sheets. The war was well and truly over and I was back in Ciwy Street. Now began the serious business of planning for the future.

Chapter 7

My New Life in HM Customs
and My Uniform Number Four

IWas lucky in that I had a job to go back to under the terms of the Resettlement Act. I was soon back in Liverpool's Liver Building working once more as 'temporary clerk' for the Ministry of Supply. Much had changed, not least a general feeling of insecurity. It soon became apparent that as we were supernumerary, we could be moved on, or even given the push, after 12 months. I was offered a transfer to the Admiralty in London or the Department of Atomic Energy at Risley near Warrington, much closer to home. This is what I chose.

It still meant a fair bit of travel – a bus into Liverpool, then a train to Warrington, then another bus to Risley. While at Risley, I applied for other jobs, some of them in the Civil Service, and took various exams. After passing one of them, I received orders to report to the water guard superintendent at Manchester Docks, in February 1950, for the job of assistant preventive officer.

Tragically, around this time, my family suffered a sad loss with the death of my brother Stephen, who had been ill for some time. He had been in the Liverpool Royal Infirmary with peritonitis but then returned home, with nothing more they could do for him. Stephen was the brightest academically of us boys and had won a place at university – Mother never got over the loss.

When I arrived in Manchester for my new job, and thus my Uniform Number Four, I walked along the dock road and asked a burly policeman for directions. I explained that I was a new entrant into HM Customs and needed to know where they were based, prompting him to say: "Oh, God help you – one of them?" I soon found myself in the Waterguard office on the docks. This was situated in an old tumble-down building, on the top floor (The bottom floor was occupied by the dock police). I was handed over to Norman Dodds, the office PO, who introduced me to Ernie Grantham, the CPO (chief preventive officer). He had a kindly manner and gave me good advice about boarding ships.

I was taken into the APO's retiring room and then a motley crew of scruffs, in dirty boiler suits and with suitcases slung over their shoulders, charged in. I had just met my first 'rummage crew'. The man in charge, dressed a bit smarter with white shirt and black tie, and with naval lieutenants' markings on his sleeves, was Sam Crumpton, our rummage PO. I was nervous, but need not have worried – they were a great bunch of lads and made me feel at home straightaway.

I was initially attached to the rummage crew (commonly referred to by seamen as the black gang). We boarded all sorts of ships, of various nationalities, newly arrived in the docks. We searched them thoroughly for smuggled goods – usually cigarettes or bottles of spirits. For my first experience of a seizure, I was with Ken Ryle and he took me down into the tonnage hatch of one of the Manchester liners. This was a sort of store place where they kept ropes and tarpaulins. He told me to poke around at one end while he went to the other. He shouted 'bingo' and called me over, having found three cartons of American cigarettes (600) and showing me where they were hidden.

Together with two colleagues, I was sent on an initial training course in London. We were put up in digs with a Mrs Stannard in Court Lane, Dulwich. She was like a second mother to us. She gave us a good breakfast and always had a huge dinner awaiting us, on our return. Half-way through the course, we had two practical sessions — visits to Tilbury, to examine passengers' baggage, and Surrey Commercial Docks, to measure deck cargo.

Back in Manchester (where we forever queried the way the regular POs did certain jobs), I boarded a Strick Line ship with the rummage crew and was tasked with searching the Indian crew's quarters. I found one of the crew lying down in a cabin smoking a 'hubbly bubbly' – a contraption comprising a vessel half full of water with rubber pipes going in and out of it. There was a mouth piece on one end and a sort of chimney on the other. He was smoking away, looking very happy, and the water was bubbling furiously. I suspected he was smoking opium. I asked him what he was smoking, but he replied: "Capstan Full Strength" – and he wasn't lying!

Among many other amusing incidents, I had to go to Eccles (by bus) and board a British coaster to deliver a 'jerque note' (inward clearing bill). Having done that, I decided to search for possible hidden contraband. I entered a crew cabin and found a coloured 'chap' lying on top of his bunk. I indicated that I needed to search his bunk, and he turned around, shedding some of his blankets. To my amazement, 'he' was a 'she' … without a stitch of clothing on. She was a prostitute – they were often to be found hanging around on ships – and I made a hasty exit, abandoning my contraband quest.

During my spell in Manchester, I was sent on detached duty four times. The longest was at Dover in the summer of 1951. I went with Bob Gray, a quiet, laid-back chap. We stayed with a Mrs Banks in a house on a road leading up to the castle. She was a chain smoker, with not the most attractive appearance, but she had a heart of gold and was an excellent cook.

Our duties mostly involved dealing with passengers' baggage. My favourite duty (8 am to 4 pm), and long before the development of today's Eastern Docks, was attending at the old 'Eastern Arm' wharf. There was only one ship – the Halladale – which sailed every morning. We travelled on the water guard bus to execute 'outward baggage' and then, once it had sailed at around 10:30 am, we had nothing to do until it returned from Calais at about 3 or 4 pm. We would sit on the beach, sunning ourselves, and then resume work – 'inward baggage' – once we saw the Halladale returning. The thing is, this never finished until after 6 pm – so we were actually due two hours' overtime! Then, twice a week, the ship did a double and on these days, we clocked up 16 hours a day – equals 'money for old rope'!

The train APO duty was also a doddle. There were two shifts – 6 am to 2 pm, and 4 pm to midnight. For the early one, you boarded the train ferry at the Western Docks at 6 am; this was the famous Pullman 'Wagonlite' from Paris to London. The train APO was given a spare cabin and patrolled the train to London, looking out for contraband that might be thrown out of the windows or doors. All I know is that we had a first class breakfast and then, on arrival at Victoria Station, we had to do a 'turn' on the exits at the baggage hall. The rest of the day was our own, and with our special train pass, we could return to Dover on any train we chose.

Closer to home, a detached duty spell at Eastham Locks involved 'processing' ships entering the Manchester Ship Canal. Everything we did had to be done while the ship was in the locks –

maximum 15 minutes. Sometimes we failed to leave the ship in time! A small boat was then sent after us down the canal and, while the ship was in motion, we clambered down a rope ladder.

At Eastham, I seemed to be on most of the time with Arthur Wiltshire, a small, friendly chap but a hard spirit drinker. There was an incident when he and I were boarding a ship in the lock and, as usual, a seaman came into the saloon to warn us that the lock gates were opening. This was our signal to get off. As Arthur began his descent down the rope ladder, and with the lock gates opened, the ship suddenly pulled out and left a 3ft gap. Everyone shouted 'don't jump', but the next thing we knew, he had dropped like a stone between the ship and the lock wall. Luckily, there was an iron rung ladder set inside the lock wall – just where Arthur had entered the water. Before we realised it, he was scrambling up the ladder, dripping wet! As his head appeared above the lock wall, his first words to me were: "Have you got my bottle?" I assured him it was safe – and, dear reader, it was not containing milk!

The Customs at Ellesmere Port boasted a 'record rummage' crew, because of the number of seizures to their name. Most of the ships using the port were oil tankers that had usually been away from Britain for two to three years at a time; hence much more smuggling. Sid Winstanley, one of the star rummagers, suggested I go and search the boat deck of a tanker that had just arrived from the Far East. He explained that a good place to search was the reels containing the rope for lowering the lifeboats. They had a sort of hollow axle where stuff could be hidden.

I went up to the first reel and gingerly stuck my 'tucstick' into the reel. It felt peculiar, a bit like tar. I unwound the rope and there in the centre were some packets of what looked like a putty-ish material. I wasn't certain of this, and so tried to attract the attention of one of the rummage crew. The PO confirmed that it was opium. I went around all the other reels – and found more packets in all of them, about 40 in all. I was excited, and the PO confirmed that this was 'a good seizure'.

I also did a small spell of relief duty at Fleetwood Fish Dock, my first experience of a fishing port. I was late arriving for my first day here, thanks to poor directions, and the PO, a Mr Yoxhall, was not amused. We had 15 bonds to ship, he announced, and I had better get my skates on. I have never known anything quite like it. We hopped on and off trawlers as if in a steeple chase. While I was left to seal up a bond locker, my boss would disappear to the next trawler. Imagine me coming out on deck, among a sea of trawlers, and wondering where on earth he was! "Over here," would come a stentorian voice from the other side of the dock.

The APOs at Fleetwood were experts at filleting and gutting fish, with their own set of knives which they kept razor sharp. And my digs offered fish in some form for every meal of the day – usually kippers for breakfast, cod for dinner and fishcakes for tea! It was a long time before I renewed my interest in fish!

What I really wanted, though, was a fixed post, and I applied for a number of these all over the country. If you didn't get a place you had applied for, you were likely to be fixed arbitrarily at any port. The two stations we all dreaded were London Port and London Airport. Luckily for me, I was posted to Goole, a small inland port in Yorkshire, on the River Ouse. On arrival, I walked down a deserted main street – it was early closing day – and ended up at a small shack on the edge of a disused barge lock. I met the office PO, Albert Barnet, a shrimp of a man, who then introduced me to the Chief Preventive Officer, Davy Donald, who was a bit of a pain. I had a short session with him, devoid of any warmth, and was then handed back to Albert to be 'processed'.

Then I met Ken Smithard, of the rummage crew, who had only recently arrived. He was from Liverpool, like myself, and had got fixed up in digs at 'Trunky' May's in Clifton Gardens. It had been arranged that I would join him there. I was given a room in the attic at the back of the house.

My time at Goole was not only a happy one but also one of considerable change in my life. The staff, apart from the CPO were like a 'family'. I spent most of my time in the rummage crew, which for a long period comprised John Baverstock, Ken Smithard and myself. Stan Coates took over from Albert Barnet later on as rummage PO. Albert, recently widowed, was a nervous character and tended to hide away, usually up in the wheelhouse, when boarding a ship to search. He was a bag of nerves if any of us got a 'seizure'. Stan Coates, ex-RAF, was the complete opposite.

Goole was a busy port with a mixed trade. When going aboard to rummage, we would go straight to the steward's cabin, dump our cases there and spread out to various parts of the ship. One of us would do the crew's cabins, one the engine room and the other the forepeak, after peak and tween decks. Goole was particularly memorable for its social life. We three – John, Ken and myself – were friends off duty as well as on. John was married to Doreen and lived in a small house on the riverbank – with Ken and me often descending on them. The drink would flow and we would all end up quite merry.

Chapter 8

**I Meet and Marry Dora...
Our Son Andrew Is Born...
And More Moves at Work.**

While I was at Goole, a civil service club was formed in the town – leading to my meeting my future wife! The idea of the club was to promote and stage sporting and social events. We attended meetings at the Odd fellows Hall and it turned out to be mostly a Customs and Inland Revenue club. John's wife, Doreen, worked in the tax office and at one of the meetings, to arrange an outing to Scarborough, she brought two colleagues – Dora Mapplebeck and Molly Longley. We all went on the Scarborough trip, to see the musical *Chu Chin Chow*, and this was the start of a friendship between Ken and Molly, and Dora and myself that led to both couples getting married.

Goole's social life was really good, especially in winter, and there always seemed to be a big dance on. We always went in a party – John and his wife, Dora, Molly, Ken and myself. It was great fun. We would end up fairly merry, but no-one ever got really under the weather.

Dora and I married at Howden Minster on June 15, 1952. The Vicar of Howden gave permission for my father to conduct the wedding service in the Minster. Ken Smithard was my best man and the reception was held in the former bishop's palace. I had managed to have some champagne brought over on one of the regular ships sailing to Boulogne. Alas, I had never drunk bubbly before and it was rather wasted on me.

We honeymooned in Penzance, Cornwall, staying in a small guest house, and then we moved into a flat in Clifton Gardens, the same road where my Goole digs had been. Much work needed doing to it and there was also a certain lack of privacy. The owner, Mrs Holderness, lived upstairs and each day had to walk through our quarters to reach the back garden where the rubbish bins were. What a carry-on!

In 1954, Dora gave birth to a baby boy, Andrew Stephen, weighing 6lbs 7oz. This naturally curtailed our social life, but I also had to get down to some serious studying in the evenings for my PO's exam, which was in two parts. I passed the written exam – adequately but not brilliantly – and got a very high mark with the oral. So, overall, I passed!

Some months later, I was promoted to PO and sent to Dover for the summer 'season'. I managed to get fixed up in the same digs as I had during my previous time there and I pulled up with two other POs in these digs – Geoff Lowther and Gerry Sharrock. I drove all the way from Goole to Dover in my dear old Ford Anglia with no problems, but it was a worry leaving Dora to cope with Andrew. Still, her parents lived close by.

Dover's busy season was well under way and the baggage halls were full. It was nerve-wracking at first, but I began to enjoy it after a while. It was excellent training and experience, and by the time I left Dover, I was quite confident in dealing with passengers' baggage. As always, there were many funny moments. For example, I asked one person to open a bag – and out popped a small monkey! It hopped, skipped and jumped all over the baggage bench. It turned out not to be a prohibited import and, apart from the general consternation that had ensued, all that remained was to catch the damn thing!

There was a small pub, The White Horse, close to my digs, run by two elderly ladies. One very hot day, I called in on the way to my digs for lunch. I was very thirsty but didn't fancy a beer, so they recommended their Kent Cider. I drank the first pint almost in one go. I ordered another – suspecting that one of the ladies gave the other a wink. This was knocked back like the first. I got up to go – and promptly sat back down again! Much to the ladies' amusement, I was sober from the middle upwards but drunk as a skunk from the middle downwards. I ricocheted along the wall at the side of the pub on the way back to my digs, where I had my leg pulled mercilessly!

I returned to Goole at the end of August, but it wasn't long before I was moved again, this time to Manchester Airport, or 'Ring way' as it was known then. It was early spring, 1958, and still very cold. I was sent to a council house on the Wythenshaw Estate, which was more like a jungle. I was put up by a Mrs Nolan, who had a nine-year-old daughter. A fire was not lit until she came home from school, and then it was only made up of briquettes – no heat at all! Mrs Nolan went out 'charring' and dinner was a hit and miss affair. One day when I came home, I was surprised to find her on the doorstep, asking me for a week's money in advance. She then gave me a ten shilling note and asked me to get some fish and chips!

I didn't stay there long. By complete contrast, I moved into 'Rodmill', a house with its own grounds in a 'posh' area of Cheadle. Mrs Snewing, who I guess was in her 30s, interviewed me and then showed me to my room – a pleasant one with French windows opening out onto the garden. Close by were a cloakroom and bath which she said was 'for my own use'. She told me my meals would be brought to my room, which had a desk. The meals were exotic for a lodger. I used to have coffee and croissants for breakfast, and I remember one day having lobster followed by strawberries and cream. All this was for just £2 10s. Actually, the food was so rich that I suffered terrible heartburn!

Breakfast time was a bit embarrassing. Mrs Snewing would bring my food dressed in a slinky dressing gown, clearly with nothing underneath! On a very hot summer's day, I was returning from duty when a voice from the garden said: "Is that you?" I walked over and there she was, lying on a sunbed – naked except for a towel (a very small one!) thrown loosely over her. She innocently asked me if I would like a cup of tea. I muttered a reply and she got up, clutching the towel, and sauntered into the house, amply displaying her pink cheeks! It occurred to me later that she might have been giving me signals (to which I did NOT respond).

We were very busy at the airport and closely watched over by Mr McKerchar, the CPO, who had an annoying habit of walking up and down behind you as you were examining baggage and slapping his legs with a pair of black leather gloves. Sometimes, I would be put on boarding duties. On arrival, aircraft crews came into our small office on the tarmac to be cleared. They often brought us kitchen left-overs from the plane, and sometimes half-bottles of wine. The food was usually pretty exotic.

After Ringway, I returned to Goole, but not for long. Just after Christmas, I was moved to Mildenhall USAF Base. This was a one-man post, more flag-flying than anything. My room was in the officers' quarters and mess, and the very first night, the phone rang at 3 am. Apparently, there was a plane landing at Lake Heath, so I had to go with Ron Hunt, the officer I was relieving, to see what it was all about. We were taken there in a staff car driven by a US major. The Yanks had a policy whereby any British personnel had to be escorted by someone 'equal in rank'.

A few days later, I was called out to board an aircraft from the States. As I walked towards the aircraft, I was stopped dead in my tracks by a Jeep hurtling towards me with its siren blaring. Then a strong spotlight was shone on me and a loudspeaker voice commanded: "Stand still, don't move. Put your hands in the air. Drop your case." Then I saw four American soldiers take up kneeling firing positions, pointing at me. I explained who I was, only to be frogmarched to their vehicle and bundled in. They took me to the Provost Marshall. It so happened, I had been drinking with him the night before. He dismissed the escort, shut the door and burst out laughing!

"It's not funny," I said.

"Err, gee, I'm kind of sorry about that," he replied, "reckon I need to make it up to you." After completing my business with the aircraft, he took me to the officers' mess and achieved total repair with a double whisky.

Truth to tell, I got on very well with the Yanks. They belonged to SAC (Strategic Air Command); these were the people who carried the atom bomb. Orders could be given at any time to bomb targets in Russia – frightening when I think about it now. The SAC boys were always having parties – usually wild – and I would be invited.

One of the most memorable parties of all, though, was organised by the British. With two other Customs officers who had joined me, plus the RAF liaison officer, we staged a British-style 'cider and cheese' party. Unknown to the Yanks, we laced their cider (but not ours) with vodka. The party didn't last long. The Yanks dropped like flies – all over the place! A colonel's wife climbed onto a table, took her skirt off and tried to sing the *Star-Spangled Banner* – only to fall off. The colonel shouted, "Stretcher bearer," and then slid under the table himself. We feared we may have gone too far, but the subsequent reaction was good. We were told it was the best party they had ever known!

Moving on again, I was appointed to a PO post at Boston in Lincolnshire, a small but busy port and one where I had applied for a fixed post. Dora had a cousin there, Muriel Anderson, and she was soon in touch with her. In a preliminary visit to the port, Dora and I stayed in Muriel's house while she and her husband were on holiday. We discovered some new houses being built in a quiet road about 15 minutes' cycle ride from the docks and we arranged to buy one of these – a detached house with a garage.

My new PO colleagues were Len Whittaker and John Dinsdale. Len made it clear that he regarded me as a rookie and would have preferred someone more experienced, but John (known as Dinny) was easy to get on with and, like me, was from Liverpool. He ate one whole raw onion a day – and pointed out that he had gone 20 years or more with no illness!

Dora and I moved to 71 Tower Road in June of that year – 1959 – and it was a big thrill, our first house and brand new. An early challenge was the back 'garden', where the ground was as hard as iron and the weeds were up to three feet high – ample for Andrew to hide in! Then it was the turn of the front garden, where a friendly neighbour advised planting potatoes to aerate the ground for a good lawn.

At work, it was a new experience to be my own boss, with an assistant to help me. It was a busy port, including a regular trade of Dutch Geist vessels delivering salad crops and then loading cattle. In summer, we had lots of timber boats, sometimes berthing seven abreast. That was quite a job if you had to visit the outside boat, jumping down on decks and clambering up walls of timber.

Dockside working was always potentially hazardous. One memorable incident was when I boarded a German ship in the locks, accompanied by APO Phil Gibb. He asked if he could search the holds before the Dockers arrived. I told him to go ahead. At the time, we were moving across the dock to the allotted berth, when the ship suddenly lurched. I thought no more about it then. We berthed and the Dockers boarded, only for one of them to rush to the saloon shouting: "Your man's had an accident." I dashed out on deck to find a crowd of Dockers peering into the hold. Someone was lowering a rope from the derrick – and Phil was lying flat on his back in the bottom of the hold, looking very white. I thought he was dead. Apparently, he had been in the tween decks when the ship was moving. He must have slipped in that 'lurch' and fallen some ten feet into the lower hold. I went with him in the ambulance and he was in hospital for several weeks. I had to phone his wife with the news, but she just laughed and said: "That's typical of him; he's always doing silly things!"

In lighter vein, I boarded a German ship and asked the captain for the usual details; he replied: "Horseshit." I checked and double-checked that I had heard correctly and eventually asked him to spell it. He did – 'Haulschidt' and I explained the meaning of the word I thought he had said. "Ja, I know," he replied, and I got the distinct impression it was not the first time he had had such a conversation!

Chapter 9

**The Loss of My Dora...
My Second Marriage...
And a New Life in Northern Ireland**

My stay in Boston, unfortunately, included one of the saddest chapters in my life. Dora became unwell with stomach trouble, and as it got, worse she was in and out of hospital several times. She didn't get any better, and I remember one Christmas – I think it was 1962 – when she was in Wyberton Hospital, just outside Boston. Andrew was staying with my parents and it was a very bleak time. A good part of Christmas Day itself was spent at that hospital.

The previous day, my spirits were particularly low when I was in a near-deserted Chinese restaurant, dining alone – and had a beautiful reminder of the true spirit of Christmas. A little old lady clambered up the stairs, clutching her shopping, and asked for a cup of tea. The Chinese waiter appeared flummoxed by this, shrugging his shoulders and returning to the kitchen. He delivered the cuppa and the lady took out her purse and asked the price. For the first time, the waiter's face broke into a big smile as he said: "Noting – Happy Klissmas!" At that, he helped her with her shopping and gently escorted her down the stairs.

Dora was eventually referred to a mental hospital in Lincolnshire, but that was a big mistake and she was sent back to Boston with a note for our GP diagnosing a lump on her parathyroid gland. She was then referred to St Bartholomew's Hospital in London, to which I went backwards and forwards by train. She eventually had to have 'gastrectomy' – partial removal of the stomach – and I was kindly offered a bed in a private ward. The end came on a Sunday after a second operation in which she suffered a massive haemorrhage.

Visiting time had just begun when the doctor asked me to leave the room for a moment. As I did so, I saw Dora's parents, and her brother John and his wife arrive. I was just giving them the latest news when the doctor asked me to come into his office – where he informed me that Dora had passed away.

My new circumstances were hard to come to terms with. When Dora had gone to 'Bart's', I had engaged an unmarried mother to 'live in' and look after Andrew, now seven. She didn't stay long and I had to advertise for someone else after Dora died. A widow, Mrs Reetham, and her ten-year-old daughter then moved in. This was a relief to me as I was now engaged in shift work, and it was a busy year at the docks.

I nonetheless joined the Toc H movement, the international charity, and put my heart and soul into it. Toc H had its origins in Belgium, at the end of the First World War. It was originally for soldiers but soon expanded to provide Christian fellowship in all classes of society and all religions. I would often do hospital visiting or go to old people's homes; I would sometimes decorate widowed pensioners' houses and tidy up their gardens. We usually ended up having quite a chin-wag, and they clearly enjoyed it.

I had been a widower for at least two years when I met Elizabeth, a widow who lived and worked in Warvick. She had three children and employed a nanny – Joy, a West Indian, with a daughter of her own – and as well as her 'extended family'. She also put up two policemen as lodgers. I was totally captivated by Elizabeth, who had previously lived in Larne in Northern Ireland. She was widowed in distressing circumstances and this was a very hard time for her. She was highly intelligent and proud, and different from any other woman I had ever met.

We were married in May 1966, at St Peter's Church, Hampton Lucy (Shakespeare country), and a village on the River Avon. It was a lovely service – with Eric, one of her policeman lodgers, as best man – and my bride looked magnificent. Guests included my parents and David, my youngest brother, and his then girlfriend Vicki. Our honeymoon began in the Albany Hotel in Birmingham, followed by various hotels in the Cotswolds.

We set up home in Boston, but I quickly realised it was unfair to expect Elizabeth to live in the home that I had shared with Dora. So we bought a house in Tawney Street, beside the park, and had some very happy times there. On Saturday nights, we would walk into the centre of town, enjoy a few schooners of draught sherry and then cross the road to the Cabaret Club, where there was always a cabaret act at 10 pm and midnight.

Coming home late one Saturday, Elizabeth shouted to me to hurry up with the key as she was desperate for the toilet. Alas, I had the misfortune to fall over a 4ft hedge alongside the path and ended up looking at the stars. I heard a distant voice saying: "Neville, Neville, where are you?" She burst out laughing when she discovered what had happened.

Even after changing houses, however, it was obvious that Elizabeth did not like living in Boston. I think she regretted leaving Warwick and I also detected some homesickness for Northern Ireland, her birth place. So I looked at the job vacancies we received at work and applied for one at Belfast's Aldergrove Airport, but this did not involve a 'crown removal', where all removal expenses would have been paid for, and so we could not afford to make that move. However, it was not long before I landed a PO job at Newry Land Boundary Patrol Station.

I personally was sad to leave Boston, where I liked the work and the town, but I knew it was important to make a new home, in a completely new place, for Elizabeth and her children. So a new stage in my life was about to begin … and little did I realize what the future held, with terrifying events that rendered Northern Ireland a virtual war zone.

Chapter 10

**We Settle in Our New Home...
But 'The Troubles' Intensify**

My knowledge of Ulster before meeting Elizabeth mostly came from my mother, whose parents came from County Londonderry. My parents knew a number of people in the Province and apparently there was even a plan to 'farm me out' with some friends in Cushendun so that they could return to Nigeria. Mother's malaria, or rather the threat of a recurrence, put paid to that.

Shortly after our marriage but before my Customs transfer, we all as a family visited Elizabeth's parents' house in Larne. Wesley and Mary Jane were a lovely couple and made me feel very welcome. I found the whole Ulster atmosphere very refreshing. After an advance 'scouting' mission by Elizabeth, we bought an old house, named Glen Villa, in Rostrevor.

I eventually took up my new post in the Newry Land Boundary Patrol Station. The office was on the third floor of an old building in Hill Street. The CPO, Stan Jeffreys, was very informal and friendly, in stark contrast to my previous CPOs. I was fixed up in digs on the seafront at Warren point, about six miles from Newry. The digs were run by two middle-aged Baptist sisters and their home was clean and comfortable.

My family eventually joined me from England, but much work was still being done to Glen Villa and so we lodged at a boarding house run by Mrs Davies. (Her property was later destroyed by terrorist action.) I had the strangest experience at Glen Villa after another evening of hard work there. I was finishing off a job upstairs when I heard a noise at the front door. From the top of the stairs, I saw a man dressed in an old-fashioned frock coat and black hat. He looked up at me and the detail of his appearance was as clear as could be. Then he suddenly vanished.

I was rooted to the spot. I eventually returned to my digs, wondering if I had been daydreaming. Then, two days later, I was sorting out some rubbish in a downstairs room there when I discovered some old photographs and postcards – and in amongst them all was an old sepia shot of that very man I had seen. There was no mistaking it. On the back was written 'Henry Lightbody' and a date. The Light bodies were former occupants of the house. Some things you just can't explain!

Back at work, I was instructed in patrolling the border. This, incidentally, is emphatically not a straight line. It weaves around all over the place – sometimes through private farm land, down the centre of narrow lanes and in one case through the centre of a shop, splitting the counter in two! I was given a patrol crew – three APOs – and a patrol car.

Technically, our job was to patrol our stretch of the land boundary from Upper Fathom, near Omeath, to County Bridge in Armagh. We were also responsible for coastline from St Johns Point to Warrenpoint and covered all shipping arriving at Warrenpoint Docks, where volumes increased substantially after port development.

I was soon out on patrol on the border – and encountered some strange situations. For instance, a farmer with fields straddling the border had built a tunnel between them and could smuggle cattle without being caught. Everyone, including police and customs, knew it was going on – but no-one ever actually saw it.

I learnt that Customs action on the border had occasionally provoked violence. Some of our staff at Newry had been involved in mild skirmishes. Alex and Bob Carey and, I believe, Hugh O'Neil, had been attacked. Little did I foresee that I would be added to the list of victims? One autumn evening, I had planned a 4 pm to midnight watch with the intention of patrolling the border at Carrickasticken near Forkhill. We were the only crew on duty that night, which was a mistake.

I had Joe O'Connor and Jimmy Campbell with me. A suspect vehicle approached and desperately tried to do a three-point turn when it spotted us, but we were just in time to block it. I went to question the four occupants, who looked pretty mean. Then I noticed a small car coming towards us and me, in my innocence, I said to the driver of the suspect vehicle: "You'd better pull into the side to let this man get past." At the same time, Jimmy moved the patrol car. The suspect driver moved to the side all right but didn't stop there. Instead, he shot over the border, making me feel a right 'eejit' (idiot).

Then their car stopped a few yards over the border and I heard men running up the road. Next thing, they were on top of me, beating the hell out of me! I fell to the ground and heard someone shout: "Kick the bastard in the head." Luckily, he didn't connect with my head, but I was caught on the shoulder and passed out. Jim called up Joe O'Connor and they rushed me to Daisy Hill Hospital in Newry, where I stayed for two or three days. I was not badly hurt – just 'shook up'.

I was off sick for about two weeks but was soon back in my normal stride. I was advised to sue Armagh County Council and received £500 compensation. We later discovered that the car I stopped and searched had come to collect a load of butter to smuggle south, and that other car was full of butter, ready for transferring.

A new IRA offensive against Northern Ireland took hold in 1970, following riots in the summer of 1969, and this was to last for a quarter of a century. The traditional targets for the IRA had always been the Customs posts on the border. These were the first tangible signs of the British presence – relatively easy to hit and escape from.

One of the first incidents I can recall was when the Killeen border post was blown up. No-one was hurt, but the staff were given only minutes to get out. This, I think, was when Bill McCullagh, PO, went up to one of the IRA gunmen, tapped him on the shoulder and said: "Excuse me, but do you mind if I go back in again to get my watch?" The terrorist's answer to this polite request has not been recorded!

IRA attacks became numerous, all over the Province, and our staff naturally grew apprehensive after the Killeen bombing and many other attacks on land boundary posts. Domestically, Elizabeth and I were settling in nicely in Glen Villa. She was now working as a housing officer with the housing trust in Belvoir, just south of Belfast, and made the long trip there daily. Her two daughters, Louann and Helen, were attending Kilbroney Primary School in the village, and the two boys, Andrew and Carlton, were now at Newly High School.

The IRA offensive intensified in 1971. The honeymoon period for the British troops was over, with snipers bullets replacing cups of tea. My parents visited us in August of that year and, after a day's visit to Armagh, we all returned to Rostrevor to find the village teeming with police, who were evidently searching for someone. Mum and Dad were quite venous – it was their first experience of 'the troubles'.

The full horror of it all was graphically brought home to me following another, more serious incident at the Killeen land boundary post. An Army patrol had been ambushed and in the ensuing gunfire two Customs staff were shot dead. Ian Hankin, a young LPM (land preventive man), was standing in the door of the post and was caught in the crossfire. Jimmy O'Neill, our irrepressible cleaner, was in a store room that caught the full force of machine gun fire. He never stood a chance.

I had to go to Killeen with my patrol crew to assist as necessary and I was horrified to see the blood-spattered room where Jimmy had been. I didn't know Ian very well, but Jimmy had cleaned our Hill Street offices every evening. The whole staff, plus officers from across Ulster, attended his funeral.

In August, 1971, internment was introduced and the IRA retaliated with many more incidents across the Province. In one incident, I was told to take a patrol crew to the Upper Fathom post and I went off accompanied by Peter McConville, my driver. We reached Dromalane, at the start of the Fathom line, when we ran into a high jacking. We were faced with a car full of masked men wielding revolvers. Peter managed a rapid three-point turn, but the terrorists drove alongside us, with their windows down and guns pointed at us.

They signalled 'abandon car', but Peter stepped on the accelerator and sped forward at a rate of knots. The terrorists fired in our direction as they pursued us; Peter mouthed obscenities, while I slithered lower and lower into my seat, muttering the Lord's Prayer. Our pursuers actually gave up the chase after a while, before we reached the main Dublin road.

The following year was possibly the worst of them all for incidents involving Customs staff and border posts. The bombing of Newry Custom House at 9:40 am on August 22 claimed nine lives. The IRA arrived at a very busy time, holding up our staff at gunpoint while they positioned their bomb. But it went off prematurely, killing four Customs officers, two of the terrorists and three lorry drivers processing entry documents. Bill Carson, a landing officer, was at his desk upstairs when the floor collapsed beneath him and he and his chair ended up on the floor below. A surveyor was blown out of his office and landed, just shaken and bruised, in another one.

With my mother and brother Stephen, who sadly passed away at the age of 18.

My Army unit at El Ballah, Egypt – extreme right end of front row (I was a sergeant).

Suez Canal from Lake Timsah.

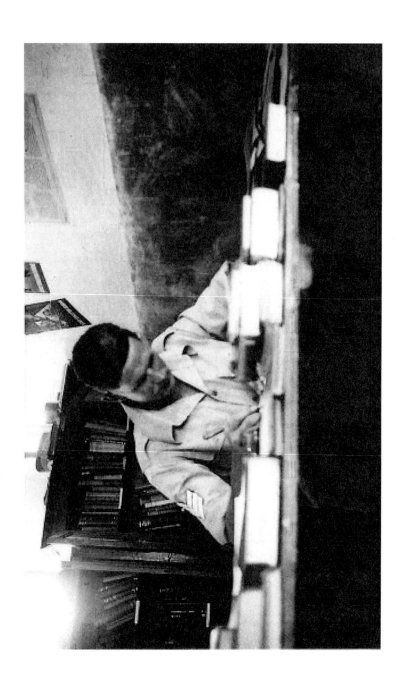

Education Sergeant for the Battalion in my office at El Ballah.

At El Ballah, Egypt (before promotion)

Together with my staff at El Ballah (second from left).

With two mates at the Pyramid of Cheops and The Sphinx.

Chapter 11

"There Is No Need to Be Afraid, Providing You Do... Exactly What We Say..."

Not long after the Newry bombing, I began the first of two interludes away from Northern Ireland, with a post at Southampton Docks, in August, 1972. We rented a house in the village of Dibden Purlieu, on the edge of the New Forest. It was about 12 miles from 'Soton' but quite close to Hythe, which had a ferry service that took about 15 minutes. I liked Southampton and my work there very much and in different circumstances we might well have stayed. Unfortunately, Elizabeth's son, Carlton, who had begun a special course in Newry, could not be catered for here and so Elizabeth reluctantly concluded that we would have to return to Newry. We had put our house there up for sale and had been actively seeking a new home in the Soton area.

We found one in Chandlers Ford and also learnt that a couple had signed the contract on Glen Villa. So we went ahead and signed the contract on 38 Valley Road, Chandlers Ford – only to discover that the couple purchasing Glen Villa had reneged on this deal, and so we were left owning two properties. So we now had to try and sell Chandlers Ford whilst returning to Rostrevor. At work, I was stationed at Soton's 29 Berth and most of my work involved boarding and storing the ferries – the Normandy ferries, operated by Townsend Thoresen (the Vikings), the P&O ferry Eagle, and the Swedish Lloyd ferry Patricia, plus a couple of French vessels. We worked in pairs and when one of these ships came in we would normally be occupied for the whole watch. Our first job after issuing pratique was to deal with the crew's manifest and take duty if necessary (it usually was). After taking an account of the ship's stores and placing them under seal, we would enjoy a leisurely breakfast in the restaurant. Then it was off to the chief steward's cabin to await arrival of stores for the next trip. The shop on the open deck of the Patricia was run by two women and we would help them lug the boxes about – for which we were invariably rewarded with perfume testers and samples! This ensured that during that period Elizabeth was most expensively perfumed! From the shop, we would descend into the bowels of the vessel to do the ship's stores, suitably refreshed by one or two bottles of lager. After lunch, it would be back to the office to write up, sign off and go home – what a life! Once, I got sent to the Queen Elizabeth II (QE2) to do crew duty, but I was not impressed by this famous ship (although I saw only a small part of her). It was the consensus in shipping circles that the French liner La France was far more luxurious. Elizabeth, meanwhile, was looking for work and became friendly with Lorna Campion, who was born in Northern Ireland and was now managing a job agency in Southampton. Elizabeth secured a good job working for the housing department in Limington, a village at the other end of the New Forest from us. On Saturday nights, we would go to The Falconers inn in Fawley for a meal and dance. The trio playing there would spot us and play *When Irish Eyes Are Smiling*. So one way and another, it was a great pity that we had to return to Rostrevor. Upon so doing in October 1973, I was posted to Killeen and Elizabeth got a job at Warrenpoint Harbour as secretary to Archie Shields, the managing director.

The troubles, if anything, had got worse – as I was forcefully reminded one otherwise quiet afternoon as I was writing up reports. The door suddenly opened and a small man with his head covered in a sort of Klu Klux Klan hood burst in. He had a gun and was carrying, what turned out to be, a bomb. He body-searched me and ordered me into a small car outside. Another masked gunman in this vehicle ordered me – pressing his gun into my neck – to crouch down on the floor and not move. As the car drove off towards the Republic, one of the gunmen said quietly: "There is no need to be afraid, providing you do exactly what we say. We know where you live in Rostrevor. You are married and have two boys and two girls. If you are tempted to inform the police, giving the full details and descriptions, we will be forced to take punitive action against you." They stopped just short of Carrickarnon ROI customs post and ordered me out. I began walking rather shakily up the road to our post, in uniform minus my cap. When I was about 300 yards from the post, there was a huge explosion – and all I immediately thought was 'My car will have been destroyed'! In the event, it was just covered in dust and rubble. The portakabin – our temporary post – had been flattened, but nobody was hurt. Another uninvited guest was a masked man who burst into the post carrying what looked like a tea tray with a pot or something on it. He told me I had five minutes to get out. This time there was a happier outcome. A bomb disposal unit came with a mechanised trolley, with robot arms attached, to sniff out the bomb, diffuse it and make it safe. In those dark, difficult days, the presence of the Army was itself deemed a danger, with the ever-present threat of their being ambushed. One evening, shortly before closing the post, I was busy writing up with Killeen's senior PO, Butch McCullagh, when an LPM shouted: "The Army are down the road; I think we ought to evacuate." 'Butch' was one of the old school who could not be diverted or corrupted in any way. Ignoring the IPM, he reached for his binoculars, looked out of the window and declared: "Good gracious; there's Jupiter." The LPM and his mates, stuck for an answer, rushed up the road like startled rabbits. I stayed on with Butch and we closed the post at the normal time, without incident. Perception is often different from reality, of course. I am sometimes asked for my reflections on 'The Troubles' from an Englishman's viewpoint. When I first arrived in Northern Ireland, in 1967, I was naturally aware of previous IRA activity, but my knowledge, such as it was, was 'sketchy' and without full understanding of the deep issues involved. During the 1930s in Liverpool, there had been some incidents that I had experienced, but they had made little impression on me. Being a Protestant coloured my outlook and, if anything, even more so for being British.

I have often thought that we are all creatures of our environment, and that our upbringing and formation of our outlook will in nearly all cases be inevitable. I quickly grasped that the Nationalists' main aim was a united Ireland, with no British interference in its running. For this to happen, all British institutions would have to be withdrawn. The IRA, who claimed to represent the Nationalists, believed these aims could only be achieved by force, and to this end they employed terrorism. IRA terrorism was not selective. It may have begun that way, but the fact is that most of their victims have been ordinary Irish people – men and women, old and young, children and even babes in arms. And what about the ordinary Protestant pro-British population and their aims. They simply want to uphold the union with Great Britain and not to surrender their sovereignty; why should they?

They look upon the Republic of Ireland as their neighbours, not their enemies. But once a neighbour attempts to interfere in your affairs, they cease to be trusted and treated as a friend. Lest I be accused of being partisan, I should make it clear that there has also been a considerable amount of terrorism by the so-called 'loyalists' (loyal to whom, I wonder?). Their activities were originally in response to IRA attacks, and in the beginning I think they genuinely believed they were defenders of the Protestant community – but there is a subtle difference between defence and retaliation. Terrorism is terrorism. Murder is murder, no matter its source or context. Time and again, we have seen that there is no solution in retaliation. There can only be accommodation. I think it is fair to say that most fair-minded Protestants would live quite happily with Catholics who accepted the sovereignty of the state as indeed they do in the rest of the UK. Conversely, I suppose most Catholics would live happily with Protestants who accepted a United Ireland and, as a result, Irish rule. But there's the rub – neither is likely to happen, at least not in my lifetime. The plantation of Ulster began in the mid-17th Century, largely involving Scots Presbyterians. A century earlier, English planters had settled, mostly in the south. The descendants of the Ulster planters are straight, honest and hard-working people. They are the most hospitable folk I know and would do anything to be helpful and charitable but the one thing they will not give up is their birth right! I return now to my own life story and to my second interlude away from Northern Ireland. In 1977, with Elizabeth's approval, I successfully applied for a PO post at Surrey Commercial Docks, on the south side of the Thames in Bermondsey. We found a house in Lanercost Road, Tulse Hill, in South East London, owned and occupied by Mr French, a widower. I moved in there, with Mr French transferring to a residential home, and once again we put our Rostrevor house on the market. Glen Villa was sold and Elizabeth and the two girls moved temporarily into Lotte Best's house at Ballyedmond, where the two boys were already living. It was a difficult time for Elizabeth. Neither of the girls was well and this delayed their move to London. They finally arrived just before Christmas. They brought with them a family 'addition' – a German shepherd puppy called Eugenie. Elizabeth herself became quite ill – I think things had got on top of her – and she spent Christmas Day in bed. She recovered and got down to the task of renovating the house, while I settled into my new work, dealing with shipping arriving at the various wharves on the Thames south bank. The river was an eye-opener. I had not been on the Thames since my initial training course in 1950. Then it was a hive of ships and boats of all types; now there was precious little activity. Another surprise came when boarding the Ellerman Wilson container ships. When I joined the Customs service, Ellerman ships meant passengers and cargo. Now they just struck me as floating hearses – just loads of big boxes, with no character. Even the captains were disillusioned. One told me: "We are no longer master mariners; we are just glorified van drivers." Another captain demonstrated what a small world it is: "I know a clergyman, called Henshaw – the Rev Ernest Henshaw – would he be any relation of yours?" This captain lived in Wallasey and when he was home, he was an active member of his local church, which my father had looked after for a while during an interregnum. Elizabeth liked London – I could always take it or leave it – but the girls could not go to the same school. Helen was admitted to St Martins-in-the-Field Girls School – quite a snooty affair – while Louann had to attend a fairly rough Comprehensive, where she was given a hard time for being Irish. Elizabeth soon found employment at the London Dungeon. Then came the news that I was on the HEO list – I was to be promoted to Higher Executive Officer once I had secured a post. I successfully applied for a VAT post in the Belfast Local VAT Office. I would have preferred a Docks post if I'd had the choice, but there were big changes going on and the Waterguard as I had known it was finished. So we had to move house once more. Elizabeth clinched a deal to buy a house in Larne owned by her friends Lucie and Fergus Kelly and we, or rather Elizabeth again, sold our house in London. We liked our new home, in Chaine Memorial Road, very much – especially its position. I loved watching the ferry, all lit up, coming in of an evening. Shortly after moving in, we had an extension built on the side of the house, followed by a second extension at the back later on. The Belfast Local VAT Office was then housed at Lisburn (moving later to permanent accommodation in Belfast Custom House). Alas, I hated VAT work! It was so different from waterguard work, which I had loved.

A good VAT man had to have a probing mind – approaching each case as though it were fraudulent. I was never a good VAT man – I was too trusting! Shortly after coming to Larne, I received sad news. My father suffered an accident in the Wallasey flat where he and Mum lived. He had fallen all the way down from the top of the stairs and was rushed to hospital by ambulance. I visited him with my mother, but he failed to recognise me. Not long after returning to Larne, I learnt that he had passed away at the age of 84. Together with Elizabeth, I attended the funeral. The church service was in Wallasey, but interment was at Anfield Cemetery in Liverpool, where my brother Stephen was buried. I think Dad would agree that he had led a fulfilling life, especially when you remember that he had been born into poverty in the city slums. For me, meanwhile, a new chapter in my life was about to be written, together with my fifth and final uniform.

Chapter 12

**My Uniform Number Five...
I Enter My Life's Final
Chapter...
And Lose My Beloved
Elizabeth**

Soon after coming to Larne, I decided to join the RUC Part-Time Reserve and thus my Uniform Number Five. I was attached to Larne Police Station and was expected to work seven or eight hours a week – usually between 7 pm and midnight and sometimes on a Saturday and Sunday. There were also courses and night classes and I had to undergo firearms training in the use of our personal hand gun (a Walther Police Pistol).

When I first attended firing practice, I thought that with my Army experience, it would be easy. For some reason, I was very nervous and did badly. I had to return for a second, much improved practice. We were supposed to carry our firearms, on duty or not, but I never did.

My duties alternated between 'walking the beat' down the main street and guard duty in the 'sangar' (the sentry box at the entrance to the police station). Sometimes we went out on mobile patrol. A crew of six or seven went out in a police van and set up vehicle check points (VCPs) on selected roads.

Almost by default, and for all that we loved our house in Larne, within three years we were on the move again. Elizabeth received word that Forestbrook House in Rostrevor, formerly occupied by the managing director of Forestbrook Mill, Mr Mcvittie, was coming on the market and would we be interested? We had a look at it, but were not all that enthusiastic; it was in a bit of a state, having been unoccupied for over a year. However, Elizabeth decided to make an 'unrealistically low' offer which, to our astonishment, was accepted.

We moved in in the summer of 1981 and were immediately faced with a lot of hard work and considerable expense. Forestbrook House, standing in an acre of ground, is possibly the oldest house in Rostrevor, having been built circa 1710. We needed extra carpets and curtains and the house had to be decorated from top to bottom. While I was bussing to Belfast every day for my work, Elizabeth would be hard at work wallpapering. Then I would help out in the evenings and at weekends. We also used up 40 tons of Sandtex to cover the whole of the outside of the house, which was well worth it, and one other big job was filling in a pit in the back garden. Apparently, Mr Mcvittie had designs on a swimming pool, but it never got finished. A fair amount of rubbish had been thrown in, but we managed to find someone to fill it in with earth. It's now covered over with grass.

The duties of a control officer in VAT were very flexible and, provided you got through your workload, timekeeping was of virtually no importance. Depending how important and 'big' a contractor was, a visit could take as much as three days or as little as half a day. Then came the writing up of the reports. Friday was the day I tackled this. The rest of the week might not see me turn up at the office at all. This freedom was, I suppose, the best part of the job – but I never really enjoyed the work. My heart wasn't in it and I just went through the motions, keeping my head above water.

Around the beginning of 1983, I got the opportunity to do a spell of detached duty at Birkenhead VAT office. There was a scheme to give, for want of better words, 'war-weary' customs officers a chance to get away from the pressures of the troubles in Northern Ireland. The Birkenhead base was a short bus trip away from where my mother lived in West Kirby. I was handed some VAT files to work on and I did some visits in Liverpool, including some old haunts, and a fair number throughout the Wirral. It's sad to recall now that this was the last time I saw my mother, although I remained in regular phone contact with her.

We had new health issues of our own. Elizabeth started attending the Royal Victoria Hospital twice a year, having been diagnosed with glaucoma. This, if not properly treated, can lead to blindness. Then, towards the end of 1983, I began suffering pains in the chest and shortness of breath. A consultant ordered me into Daisy Hill Hospital, where I had the 'shock treatment'. This was designed to restore my regular heartbeat but it didn't work and ever since I have been on a course of digoxin. I was off work for a short while, but when I returned it was obvious that I wasn't the 'full shilling'.

My surveyor, Billy Bell, suggested I make moves towards early retirement. I had less than a year to go anyway, so would not lose out on pension rights. I was more than ready to go – travelling to Belfast had become quite a drag – and so I retired from HM Customs and Excise after 33 years' service. It would be nice to say I viewed my going with sadness and nostalgia, but that would be dishonest. Now, I am sometimes asked what I find to do all day, but I am never bored and I sometimes feel I have less leisure time than before!

Around the time of my retirement, Elizabeth's health problems were worsening. She needed special treatment for her glaucoma to control the pressures at the back of her eyes. From time to time, the pressures alternated, sometimes reaching a dangerous level. The regular regime of eye drops seemed to have held things in check, but it was a constant worry. On top of this, she also now required hearing aids.

From the early 1990s onwards, I began to be more aware that I was 'getting old' (perish the thought!). I was also acutely aware of Elizabeth's increasing disabilities and realising that my ability to help her was inadequate. Fortunately, we lived in a comfortable house, which, thanks to Elizabeth's foresight and determination, had benefitted from a number of improvements. For all that, though, there was no denying that it was no longer ideal for us in our new circumstances. It had a lot of stairs – and the toilet was at the top of the house!

We began to think about moving to a smaller, more manageable home. We looked at various properties, mostly in the Larne area, and put our Forest brook house on the market. Among various viewers, the one family to express serious interest were the Haddens from Portadown. They made an offer, which we accepted.

We viewed a wooden bungalow in Branch Road, Drains Bay, Larne. It was 100 yards from the coast road, in a 'private' position and with a lovely garden bounded by a babbling brook that meandered to the Irish Sea. The sellers were an odd couple, with the man, Mr Callaghan, having served 'time' for robbery. He had installed the most sophisticated security system I had ever seen. Our offer was accepted and we moved in – now living close to Mary, Elizabeth's sister, and her family.

Our new home suited us in so many ways. We regularly took the dogs to Carnfunnoch along the coast, where there was a car park on the sea edge. Rosie loved clambering over the rocks after the seagulls! I have often wondered why we didn't stay and settle down here, and I simply have no answer to that.

In a year's time, we were planning to return to Rostrevor because we discovered that a new housing estate was being built on the Hilltown Road, to be called Mourne Wood. We moved into a four-bedroom house with a double garage and large back garden in Kilbroney Road – where I am still living – in August, 2000. There was much to do, so I set about constructing a nice garden, planting trees and shrubs, and various roses and other plants. Shortly after moving in, we decided to have a conservatory built on to the dining room and we were delighted with it. Elizabeth loved sitting in there in fine weather, looking out onto the back garden and at me mucking about doing various jobs.

On reflection, we had both now begun our 'last chapter'. Elizabeth's health was worsening, and while we were in Larne she had in fact undergone surgery (vulvectomy) in Antrim Hospital. When she was discharged, she developed shingles and we had nurses visiting for a while. After we had settled in Mourne Wood, she was registered disabled and we were able to get her a stair lift, which was a big help. We also engaged carers.

I began to feel that Elizabeth needed a break, so we decided to go to Florida to visit Helen and Fionbar. We stayed with them for nearly four weeks – their bungalow was a nice, 'roomy' property in Spring Hill. The weather was great and Cynara, who turned out to be a real water baby, accompanied us on visits to various beaches and places of interest. The one thing that did not impress was the restaurants, which were absolute rubbish! They made us realise how good Irish restaurants and cafes are!

I'm sure that trip did Elizabeth the world of good. Back home, though, my own health was about to take a turn for the worse. In April 2004, I suddenly felt really rough with pains in my chest. Elizabeth urged me to see our GP, and Dr McLoughlin sent me to Daisy Hill Hospital by ambulance with a suspected minor heart attack. I was there for several days and then transferred to Belfast's Royal Victoria Hospital. After tests, I was given to understand that I would probably be having a 'by-pass'.

I was prepared for an operation (an angiogram, I think). They stuck a probe through my groin. This went right up to my heart with the aim of clearing the arteries leading to it and then implanting 'stents'. A young consultant drew me a sketch of my heart and the connecting arteries, highlighting the location of the blockage. He said it would be too dangerous to deal with the blocked arteries, as they were too close to the heart, and that subsequent treatment would need to be 'medical' – tablets, in other words. Shortly after returning home, I was back in Daisy Hill Hospital for review of my medical dosage. I was soon back home again – knocking back 15 tablets a day! The initial effect was chiefly exhaustion. I don't suffer much from chest pains any more – just occasionally – and my angina necessitates use of a spray on my tongue.

Elizabeth, meanwhile, was being attended to by carers three times a day. Even so, for a short period we were still able to visit the market in Newry on Thursdays and Sainsburys on Fridays. I was now moving her around in a wheelchair. She liked going to the market and had her favourite stalls – Leila's Bric-a-Brac and the Indian couple's 'Gulzar'.

Alas, in August of that year, her health became even worse. The carers spotted a nasty rash on her stomach and she was sent to Belfast's Musgrave Hospital, where I was shocked to be told by her consultant, Mr O'Brien, that she was 'critical'. After signs of improvement, she was sent home on provision that she slept downstairs, with a hospital bed and special chair supplied. The dining room became her bedroom. The carers now came four times a day.

The rash persisted and in November it was diagnosed as cellulitis. She was taken back into Daisy Hill Hospital, with her condition ultimately diagnosed as septicaemia. I was fully aware of the serious nature of this, but her death on the evening of November 26 was unexpected and came as a severe shock to me. I had been at her bedside in hospital, along with Helen, but had to go home for some reason. Helen returned home later that evening, burst into tears and exclaimed: "She's gone."

The reality was difficult to accept. I loved her dearly, but even more importantly she was such a good friend. We always talked to each other, with no 'silences' between us. I have so many happy memories to sustain me. Some of the happiest were of our dances at the Ballyedmond on a Saturday night. She was a beautiful dancer but I was never much good until I met her!

Life has since completely changed for me, but I have been very fortunate. Both daughters – and I do genuinely regard them as 'my' daughters – are very helpful to me. My own health has further deteriorated, as is only to be expected, with my heart disease forcing me to slow up. I have to accept that there are quite a few things which I can no longer do.

One of my pleasures now is my renewed association with Andrew and his family. He suffered the sad loss of his own wife, Mary, a few years ago and, like me, has had the closeness of his son Andy and his three lovely daughters, Emma Jane, Jennifer and Amy. Andrew phones me regularly to check if I need anything and, whenever he can, takes me to collect my pension and odd items of shopping. Another joy for me has been seeing Louann's baby girl Jessica, especially as I have been able to recognise in her a distinct likeness to Elizabeth. Sadly, it has turned out that Jessica has an advanced form of autism. This occasionally causes a violent reaction, making her scream and even punch herself. I am concerned at the effect the consequent worry and stress must be having on Louann.

Chapter 13

**So Many New Interests as
I Adapt to Life on My Own
and a Delightful School
Experience**

Losing a dearly loved wife and coming to terms with living on your own is undeniably difficult and life-changing, but so much depends on your attitude. In my case, I have acquired a great many new interests, which have all helped keep my mind active.

For some years now, I have been making my own wine. This is a hobby that requires much care and precision; otherwise, the end product can be rubbish! I began by making wine with concentrated grape juice, but later produced from an assortment of fruits grown in the garden, such as blackberries, blackcurrants, apples and pears. The whole process, from initial fermentation to final bottling, fascinates me. Whilst not achieving the highest standard, my wines to date have at least been satisfactorily consumed and not poured down the kitchen sink!

Another new hobby for me is collecting coins. I now have quite a large collection; some are pure gold (22ct) and some silver, with the value of both recently increasing. I have to be careful because this hobby is quite expensive. As I approach my tenth decade, I have suddenly developed a most unexpected interest in history and archaeology. Both would have bored me stiff, when I was younger! I now look forward to the arrival of magazines covering these subjects, despite my gradually deteriorating eyesight that requires the use of a magnifying glass.

For some years, I have been attending the Presbyterian Church in Rostrevor. Although I was raised by my parents in the Church of England, I am happy to join with like-minded Christians in the worship of God. Some might ask why I never attended the Church of Ireland in our village. The simple answer is that Elizabeth was a Presbyterian and to me it was quite natural to go to church with her. I have increasingly felt that my faith in God is based simply on the Gospel of Jesus Christ. Churches, chapels and cathedrals are all places where we can gather together in a true atmosphere of Christian worship, but God's presence is not confined to a single church. I believe fervently that God is within me. The congregation of Rostrevor Presbyterian Church have shown me nothing but kindness and friendship, led by the Minister, David Temple, and not forgetting Terry and Marie Clare, Bob and Sheila Curry, God bless them.

Shortly after Elizabeth passed away, I was introduced to the Rostrevor Lunch Club. Now I look forward to going there every Tuesday and meeting up with a great bunch of people. We are all classes and creeds and there is always much laughter and leg-pulling. On top of it all, we have a really good, cheap lunch, along with numerous cups of tea! Canon Jamieson and Bridle do an amazing job organising everything, with various forms of entertainment plus summer excursions.

Whilst family relationships have always been important to me, living on my own has made me more aware of my responsibilities as head of the family. In particular, my son Andrew has become more important to me and I rely on him a lot. There was a period in my life, which I deeply regret, when I had little contact with him and his lovely family. I got that badly wrong and I am now trying to make amends for my mistakes.

Away from family matters, I have even notched up an achievement as a public speaker! Baroness Thatcher, who was Prime Minister at the time of the Falklands Conflict in 1982, died in April 2013 and not long after this I was invited to address pupils at Jordan's school in Rathfriland. I received this invitation via Louann, who told me that the headmaster, Mr Vance, had shown an interest in my wartime memories.

I certainly had a great many memories from the Second World War, but was a little wary, and even a tad nervous, at giving a talk to schoolchildren. I feared they would not be interested in what I had to say about a period in my life of more than 70 years earlier. In the event, I need not have worried. Louann, accompanied by Cynara, picked me up and drove me to the school, having first ensured that I was wearing my regalia – that my blazer was covered in an assortment of 'iron work' (medals).

On arrival at Iveagh Primary School, the school Jordan attended, I received a touching welcome from the head. He introduced me to his teaching staff, who made a big fuss of me and gave me a cup of tea. I was then escorted into the hall, where the children were respectfully seated. I recounted as many memories as I could, to the best of my recollection. On completion, I invited questions – and was amazed when a forest of hands shot up. All sorts of sensible questions were asked, and at the end of it all, I felt quite a glow of satisfaction that it had gone so well.

The next day Louann presented me with two letters. One was signed by three girl students thanking me for such an interesting talk and adding their favourable comments. The other was a letter of gratitude from the Headmaster accompanied by a bottle of red wine! The letter from the little girls was particularly touching.

Signed Emily, Rebecca and Elizabeth, from Primary years 6 and 7, it read:

"We would like to say a big thank you for coming to Iveagh to talk to Primary 6 and 7 on the 15th of April. It was very interesting to hear about how the war started, developed and ended. When you were asked to describe the war in one word, you said 'needless' and we were taken by surprise as it was not an expected answer.

When you told us about the bomb beside your house and all your lucky escapes, it made us think just how gory the war really was. We were fascinated to hear about how you risked your life and in return you were honoured with medals which you really deserved. Your talk made us reflect on what terrible things happened in the past. Once again, we thank you."

This, as I write, is one of the very latest 'highlights' in my life as it continues its 'final chapter'. As mine progresses through its twilight years, I reflect how here were 'new', young lives, for whom the stories I recounted must have seemed not so far removed from the grey pages of history books and sepia photographs of old. And yet, in our own way, with all those hands raised in curiosity after I had finished talking, we had a meeting of minds. They wanted to know so much more, and I was so keen for them to share and learn from my own experiences of so long ago. Life, I was beautifully reminded, GOES ON!

Addendums

The Pet Years

I had little interest in animals before meeting Elizabeth. When we married, she had a small Jack Russell terrier called Honey. She was given to a farmer after a police warning – Honey was too fond of chasing cyclists, prompting complaints aplenty.

Shandy the cat came with us to Northern Ireland, but did not settle at Glen Villa and disappeared into the mountains. We had a succession of cats here. Jasper had a habit of climbing up the clothes pole and teetering at the top. Psychiatric treatment was eventually required.

While we were still in Boston, Shandy ran amok while we were away and left the house in a dreadful mess. Elizabeth declared that lit would have to be put down. I took Shandy in a box to the vet's and paid for the sad service, although the receptionist had enquired: "Oh dear, what a shame; do you have to?" I returned home with the empty box, only to discover that Elizabeth was having second thoughts. Could I return to the vet's post haste to prevent the execution? I returned with the box and asked if I was too late. The vet himself came in and said: "You are a very lucky man. I kept putting off the job because quite frankly I didn't want to do it!" He gave me my money back and there was much rejoicing back home at the return of the prodigal cat.

Madame Minette was a very lovable and affectionate toy poodle. She came with us when we moved to London and was accompanied by Eugenie, the German shepherd dog puppy. Eugenie got a severe electric shock when she nibbled at a cable – which she never repeated!

These two came with us to Lame when we returned to Northern Ireland, but Madame became ill and eventually blind. She died virtually in Louann's arms. We got another poodle, but tragically this one only had a short life, being run over by a motor bike on Forestbook Road.

Bessie, an Afghan hound, had a habit of running away and one day it seemed she had gone for good. After about seven days without a sighting, Elizabeth met a woman who was a bit 'fey' and who told her that Bessie was still alive but that she would die if she wasn't found by the next day. Lo and behold, Louann turned up with her the next day. It was only just in time, but Bessie recovered and went on to give birth to a healthy litter. Louann kept two of them – Farrah and Martin – and ended up showing both dogs, with me chauffeuring to various dog shows across Ireland. Farrah even appeared at Crufts.

We lost Martin in very unpleasant circumstances. He escaped from our lower yard and was involved in an incident in the field next door, with dogs attacking sheep. Men were shouting and running in the field and Martin was shot at close range, full in the head. I had the sad task of carrying his body back to the house, where I buried him amongst the trees.

Eugenie died after developing arthritis in her rear legs. We saw her alive for one last time as we returned from shopping one day. I went straight to the stables, where she was lying on a rug. She raised her head to look at me, but when I returned from another visit to the car she was dead. It was as if she had waited for us to come back from shopping so that she could say goodbye.

I have had no dogs since Elizabeth died. With the rapid deterioration of my own health, I realised I could no longer look after dogs properly.

Family Relations

My father would often take me to visit his mother, who lived with his sister Bessie in Stanfield Road, Everton. They had no indoor toilet. The WC was half-way down the back yard. One of the two downstairs rooms was 'the parlour', a sort of holy of holies, where you were never allowed in unless you were a clergyman or a doctor.

The living room was dominated by a large black-leaded stove and a sofa of imitation leather, and my Aunty Bess's weekly chore was to black-lead that stove. I was very fond of my Grandma and discovered many years later that her maiden name was Anne Neville and I had been christened after her.

I never knew my mother's parents, who died before I was born. They came from Ulster but moved to Liverpool, where my mother was born. Her family consisted of six girls and one boy – Belle, Lizzie, Tish, Mag, Nan, Georgina and Robert. Dad's family consisted of three boys – John, Isaac and Ernest (Dad) and four sisters, Annie, Kate, Mag and Bessie. John was a stretcher bearer at the Battle of the Somme and died shortly after the end of the First World War.

John's wife had been a Red Cross nurse in France, where they had originally met. She was my Aunt Mary, from Armagh, and they had one daughter, Rosemary. The last time I met Rosemary was in Egypt of all places. She had joined the WAAF and been sent to Cairo.

My closest aunt was Auntie Nan, my mother's sister married to my Uncle Fred. They had four children, Vivien, Kenny, Enid and Eric. Enid died quite young – roughly the same age as my brother Stephen and from a similar illness.

My Auntie Belle was my mother's oldest sister, married to my Uncle 'WY' (short for Wyburg) and they kept a pub on Belmont Road. He fought in the Battle of the Somme and suffered serious facial wounds that made him ugly. He was leading his battalion when all the officers had been killed, and was awarded the MC (Military Cross).

My Auntie Mag also had four children, Charlie, Douglas, Joan and Edith. The only one we knew well was Joan, who often baby-sat for us. Of the others, Charlie went into Liverpool City Police, Douglas joined the Royal Artillery in the war, and Edith was in the Women's Military Police.

At the beginning of the Second World War, my grandmother went to live with my Aunt Annie and Cousin Evelyn in Childwall. She died after falling off a chair, when she had been trying to fix some curtains. My Aunty Bess had a good position as a bookbinder at Wallasey Library. While living with my grandmother, she would regularly come to our house in Feltwell Road on a Saturday night for a bath.

My Uncle Ike (Isaac) was the manager of a printing firm called Brakells in Liverpool city centre. I was fascinated to watch him putting gold lettering on heavy ledger covers. He used pure gold leaf that was spread over the cover. Then heavy metal letters which had been pre-heated were stamped on the gold leaf. The excess leaf was rubbed off with a ball of wax.

Auntie Kate had two daughters, who both joined the Civil Service, considered prestigious work. Both later moved to Canada and got married. Aunty Kate, who had been widowed, joined them later.

Aunty Annie was the oldest in Dad's family. She was an avid Liverpool supporter and knew all the players' names, along with all their good and bad points. She lived into her 90s. Her oldest son was my cousin Harold, who lost his job in a shipping agents' office on Liverpool Docks in the Depression after the First World War. He picked himself up and opened a small corner shop in the city, not far from where we lived.

USA Visit

In the summer of 1987, Elizabeth and I visited my brother David and his wife Vicki at their home in Hockessin, Delaware. David was a biochemist and Vicki was in a sort of hostess job at Newcastle Airport. We were met by David and a friend – who were several hours late! – And we were then driven through the worst torrential rain I had ever known.

David and Vicki's house was large and spacious – typically American – and mostly timber-built. David took some time off from work and drove us around to various places of interest. These included Baltimore, with its thriving harbour and, not least, a large aquarium with all sorts of sea creatures, even sharks and whales! We also went – on our own, by train – to Philadelphia. We visited the building that exhibits the Peace Bell', which I believe was presented by our own Queen. While waiting on Wilmington Station for the train, Elizabeth had a fascinating conversation with a local police officer – who informed her that he had relatives living in Northern Ireland.

Possibly our most enjoyable outing with David and Vicki was a cruise on the Delaware River, complete with meal, music and dancing. That was great fun. A most unusual experience was found in a restaurant close to Newcastle Airport. The theme was an officers' mess at an RAF base during the Battle of Britain. There was mock bomb damage and sandbags and an intercom occasionally playing Winston Churchill's 'Never in the field of human conflict...' speech. Then we would hear 'Squadron scramble' – Vector Angels 7. Bandits approaching 3 o'clock. We had a terrific buffet breakfast here, washed down with much Californian sparkling wine. I declined to ask for a cup of tea – I don't think I could have pronounced it!

Homeward bound once more, David took us to Kennedy Airport and on the way we stopped off at Staten Island to take the ferry to New York, sailing past the Statue of Liberty. We actually left it all a bit late, catching our plane with just ten minutes to spare!

Farewell, Mum

In the early hours of September 13, 1993, my mother passed away peacefully at the great age of 96! Shortly before her death, Gordon, who had been living with her, had gone for a short break to Hong Kong. My cousin Joan, who had a key and was in the habit of regularly calling around, found her on the bedroom floor. She was half under the bed, where she had fallen. Joan and her husband Len got an ambulance and Mum was taken to Arrowpark Hospital in Birkenhead, where she died a few days later.

She had lived a good life of 'service' – as a missionary and midwife in Nigeria, and later as Vicar's wife and leader of the Mothers' Union. She was a good mother to my brothers and me. Remarkably, her mind had remained completely alert and she had retained a sense of humour right to the end, amply expressing her northern roots!

Tragedy

Not long after Colin and Louann's wedding in 1996, a tragic accident occurred. I took a phone call in the early hours to learn that John White, Helen's close friend, had died suddenly in Amsterdam. We did not break the news to her until the next morning, and she took it badly. It was a complete shock. It appeared that his brother discovered his body in their flat. John had suffered a fatal heart attack.

Elizabeth and I were very fond of John, and we had expectations that they might have married one day.

Our Magnificent Queen

As I write this, it is the year of the 60th anniversary of Queen Elizabeth's Coronation in 1953. At that time, I was sewing as an APO in Goole. I was in bed, as I was on night duty, but was anxious to listen to the service on the radio (very few people had televisions then). I borrowed a radio set and listened to it all whilst lying in my bed. It was such a moving ceremony, accompanied by very uplifting music. I remember one of the anthems played was Handel's *Zadoc the Priest*, and Nathan, the prophet, anointed Solomon King – and all the people shouted and said, "God Save the King." One especially exciting moment came just after the Queen was crowned by the Archbishop of Canterbury, John Fisher, when the congregation cried in unison: "Vivat Regina; Vivat Regina Elizabethan." In those 60 years that have followed, the Queen has set an amazing example in showing the whole world, again and again, just what a perfect British monarch, and what a wonderful lady, she truly is. Long may she reign!

Another USA Visit

May 15, 2008, saw the start of another visit to the United States for me. Helen, accompanied by Cynara, took me to Dublin Airport to catch the 2.35 pm flight to Philadelphia, due to arrive there at 5:10 pm. It was an American Airways plane and I had a comfortable journey.

When I boarded, I was shown to an 'aisle' seat, but shortly before we took off a stewardess came to me and pointed to some seats on the opposite side that had not been occupied. She suggested I might be more comfortable there, explaining that I could stretch out and have a nap! I thought that was very considerate of her – and suspected I would not have received the same attention on a British Airways plane!

David was there to greet me on arrival at Philadelphia and I was impressed by his early 18th Century house, in East Fourth Street, Newcastle. I was given a bedroom at the rear, overlooking the back garden. Attached to the bedroom was a veranda in which I was able to stretch out on one of the folding beds. The back garden was Janice's pride and joy. It included the most amazing iris plants I had ever seen. Half-way down the garden, there was an archway with clematis growing up it.

My 'itinerary' included visits to the homes of Rebecca and Matthew plus a house party at Vicki's house. This was quite a large one, in a 'posh' part of town, and there was a large crowd there enjoying drinks and nibbles. On both Sundays, I went with David to the local Episcopalian church, which was apparently very old. We took Holy Communion and David, as a sideman, did the collection.

The day before my return home, David's neighbours, Bert and Jean, invited us to dinner. They were a lovely couple (Bert has since passed away). The two weeks had gone by in a flash and before I knew it I was flying back to Northern Ireland. Andrew met me and took me back to Rostrevor.

Christmas Memories

I have some very clear – and fond – memories of how we celebrated Christmas; when I was a young lad in Liverpool. It was a very busy time in our house. For Dad, as Vicar of Polycarp, it was possibly the busiest period of the year. For a start, there always seemed to be a lot of funerals, which meant we saw very little of him.

Christmas in our home was very much a celebration of the birth of Christ – the Star in the East, the Wise Men, the Shepherds in the Fields, and the Babe in the Manger. To me as a boy, the whole Nativity story was fascinating. Nowadays, I miss all this very much.

The build-up to Christmas didn't really start until the beginning of December, unlike the present day (2013), when we are first 'reminded' about Christmas sometime in October! A few days before Christmas, Dad took us out into Liverpool, to go round the shops. This inevitably included the 'Grotto' in Lewis's and thus accosting the great bearded man himself – Santa Claus! Whether or not we believed in Father Christmas was totally irrelevant! We were then taken to Cooper's in Lord Street, where we enjoyed a slap-up dinner in the restaurant upstairs. Waffles and syrup was our favourite pudding. Dad knew one or two of the assistants here – I think they may have been parishioners – so he was always very well treated. Mother, meanwhile, would be getting on with everything – making hay while the sun shone! We were out of the way and peace reigned for her!

Christmas morning itself was usually hectic. We had to be up early because Dad had early Communion to celebrate the night before. My mother would select three old pairs of her stockings (well laddered!) and she and Dad would then stuff them with an assortment of items consisting of a cardboard trumpet, a bag of chocolate coins, a sugar mouse, and an apple and orange. Opening those stockings – usually no later than 3 am! – was excitement personified. Later on in the day, we would be presented with our main presents.

We all went to Christmas morning service, which I have to say I enjoyed mainly because of the carols and the Christmas story. Mother was always anxious to get home after the service because the dinner would have been left on a low light. (It had been part-cooked on Christmas Eve.) Christmas dinner was traditional – turkey followed by plum pudding and then mince pies (of which my Mum made a great many!).

The King's Broadcast (George VI) on the radio was the high point of the afternoon. When they played the National Anthem, my mother always stood to attention! And we boys had to follow suit. Preceding this broadcast was a *Round the World* programme. It linked all the countries of the British Empire with special Christmas messages and reports of how the big day was being celebrated. This was always very interesting. We had no TV then, but really we enjoyed our radio just as much as we now enjoy our TV – I sometimes think even more so! There was the inevitable Dickens 'Christmas Carol', and editions of 'ITMA' and 'Band Wagon'.

Of the Christmas music at that time, Handel's Messiah was a big favourite (and it still is) and on Christmas Eve, I never missed the Festival of Nine Lessons and Carols. While I was listening to this, Mother would be busy stuffing the turkey and keeping an eye open for the mince pies. Those delicious cooking smells blended well with the music!

Christmas nowadays is totally different. It seems to start in the shops in the early autumn, but come New Year's Day it's all over. When I was a boy, we really observed the 12 days of Christmas – with January 6 (Epiphany) being the last day. I wonder if Christmas, as I knew it, is gradually disappearing altogether. It certainly appears to be.

God rest ye very gentlemen!
May nothing you dismay.
Kevnevnber Christ, Our Saviour
Was born upon this day.

Sir Winston Churchill

One person for whom I have a particularly high regard, and who undeniably had a major influence on my life, albeit 'at arm's length', is someone I never even met! But how could anyone deny the influence on my life, and on so many millions of others, of the late Sir Winston Churchill? It is an influence which I feel compelled to acknowledge here.

His role as Prime Minister and wartime leader – in the Second World War – is literally the stuff of history. In this period, he truly came into his own. He achieved the mantle of greatness – despite the fact that, as a boy, he apparently did not impress his teachers! Between the two world wars (1914–18 and 1939–45), he was regarded, at least by most of his fellow politicians, as being very much 'in the wilderness'.

He had fallen out with the Conservatives and had established something of a reputation as a warmonger'. I have always felt this was because of visits he had made to Germany, when he personally witnessed the build-up to hostilities and the dramatic increase in that country's military strength. An even more striking factor, again witnessed first-hand by Churchill, was the power wielded over the German people by the new Nazi party. The people were still reeling from the failures of the First World War. Churchill must also have witnessed the consequent financial and economic breakdown. Older people will recall, too, the Treaty of Versailles and its devastating effect on Germany as a whole.

The Second World War was basically caused by the terms of a treaty with Germany being broken. Poland was invaded and Britain was 'honour-bound' to come to its aid. Neville Chamberlain, Prime Minister at the time, made his historic announcement of the declaration of war with Germany on Sunday, September 3. He subsequently attempted to form a coalition government, but this turned out to be a failure. Cutting a long story short, Churchill was eventually considered to be the only man fit to lead, and Chamberlain finally resigned.

Right from the start, Churchill took charge. He formed a coalition, with Clem Attlee, the Labour leader, as his deputy. Ernie Bevan, the great union leader, was Minister of Labour – a great choice! – And Herbert Morrison was Home Secretary. Churchill led from the front, as they say; he wasn't one for delegating if he could avoid it. Among other things, he became famous for his memos to the various heads of organisations and to military chiefs. Memorably, they always began with 'Action This Day'. Anyone receiving such a memo knew they could not put off the required action until tomorrow!

This was one of Churchill's greatest attributes – to motivate people into action and to give them a great sense of purpose. He hand-picked the people he trusted and admired. One of them was his appointment of Lord Beaverbrook, head of the *Daily Express,* as Minister of Aircraft Production, at a time when new aircraft were badly needed. This turned out to be an excellent choice. Lord Beaverbrook was a pugnacious man – he was renowned for getting things done.

Perhaps Churchill's greatest characteristic was his ability to communicate with the 'ordinary people' of Britain in such a way that he was trusted as a father, and in some ways, genuinely idolised. His speeches, heard by the majority of people on the radio, are endlessly re-quoted and have become very much a part of this nation's history. The retreat from Dunkirk was a cause of despair for many, and even followed in some quarters by apathy, but Churchill somehow managed to rally the nation with his legendary oratory – "We will fight on the beaches … we will never surrender …"

At the height of the Battle of Britain, and after visiting an RAF headquarters, Churchill jotted down some notes on a scrap of paper. They were to be the foundation of one his most famous speeches, which included the immortal lines: "Never before in the field of human conflict, has so much been owed by so many to so few." The men to whom he referred – the surviving Battle of Britain fighter pilots – were proud to be referred to in later years as 'The Few'.

Churchill made a great many memorable speeches, and among those which made a particularly strong impression on me was one he made at the end of the North African campaign, when Montgomery's 8th Army joined up with the American 2nd Army. He told the House of Commons: "This is not the end. It is not even the beginning of the end. But it is perhaps the end of the beginning."

On a much lighter note, I was told the story of how Lady Astor, a close friend of the Churchill's, was giving a party during which the great man, as usual, had consumed a few too many! Lady Astor confronted him and in a rather loud voice exclaimed: "Winston, you're drunk!"

Churchill focussed on his accuser and replied: "Madam, you're ugly, but tomorrow I will be sober!"

At the end of the war, Churchill was discarded, for want of a better word. The Labour Party won the next General Election, mainly with the votes of returning soldiers, and Clem Attlee became Prime Minister. Churchill had completed his task. He had accomplished what he had set out to do. He had led Britain to victory in war and would no longer need to display his famous 'V' sign. Unlike a former famous Englishman, he was not a 'man for all seasons'. Churchill himself, I am sure, would have acknowledged that. Although he always indicated that he would not accept a peerage, King George VI conferred on him a knighthood and he became one of the Knights of the Garter. In so many ways, not least as a character, Churchill was a colossus on the stage of world history.

Ken Crossley, Spiderman Rowan, Mrs -------- and Yours Truly.

The rummage crew, better known by seamen as the 'Black Gang'.
The PO is the officer on the right sporting two stripes.
Left to right: John Baverstock, Yours Truly, Ken Smithard, PO (name not recalled).
All dead, except me.

Official British Customs 'agent' based at Milden hall, USAF.
Me with a couple of my American 'buddies'.

Emerging from a hold after searching for contraband.
(I didn't find anything.) PS: Notice the jemmy!

At Manchester Airport, circa 1957
Left to right: me (PO), Eric Morton, Ted Capstick

Our home in Rostrevor, Co. Down – "Forestbrook House."

My brother David's wedding to Janice, circa early 1980s

With Elizabeth on holiday in America

My wedding to Elizabeth in 1963, with members of the family and assorted friends

With my son Andrew and his family. (His wife Mary had passed away some years earlier.)
Left to right: Andrew, Andy, Jennifer, Emma, Jane and Amy with me at the front, sitting.

A special indoor street party took place in Rostrevor Presbyterian Hall recently, featuring war-time memorabilia to celebrate the publication of extracts form the memoirs of Sergeant Neville C Henshaw Royal Corps of Signals. Pictured l-r are Tommy Todd, Chairperson British Legion Kilkeel, Elizabeth Hudson, Jim Hudson, all Ex Service British Legion, Rev David Temple and Neville Henshaw. 10W23N247

Laying the wreath on Remembrance Day, 2011,

in Rostrevor Presbyterian Church.

'Conscript Youth Lost'

I am conscript fresh faced ten years and seven, eager youth full of vigour. I want to chase the local honeys, knock back a pint or two with my mates, hailing from iconic 'pool of life' ...

Under mercury swift and sure I am proficient, trained, obedient to my country's call, fit for battle, enduring war, my unit sent May 1944, Gosport strutted in secret descent, operation 'Overlord'

Hey lads, where are we going now? It's Monday 6th of June. On board an LST packed in like bewildered cattle ready for slaughter, we lit a smoke while Henshaw cracks a joke; the air erupts with rings of nervous laughter.

The veil is lifted, eerie silence befalls us, skyline exploded blazed with reddish black, orange hues. Normandy beckons battle cry, overwhelming, deafening noise, I stumble, wade heavy bare anchored aimless down.

Enveloped by unforgiving sea, hauled out of the water by a comrade in arms still clutching my rifle, my feet weighed heavy like ploughing farrows underfoot.

Golden sand inviting no-one, bloody red, three of my mates lay strewn dead. Terrified, shaken rabbit stare uttering Lord's Prayer gasping thoughts cloaked with parents love and blessings.

Officer yells, "Keep moving soldier," hunting me, driving me on riffle cocked, shell explosion shrapnel pierce my skin like unyielding sabre, smell flesh burning, fuel pumped forward going,

German fortification, relentless fire spewing like dragon, I evade clambering up into the abyss still earth bound a job to do, linesman fluent in French and German, communicate this, grateful to be alive!

By Louann (nee Henshaw) Blair

This is a poem I wrote about my dad on D-day landings on Gold Beach called 'Operation Overlord'.